HOW TO
HANDLE A
CROWD

HOW TO HANDLE A CROWD

THE ART OF CREATING HEALTHY AND DYNAMIC ONLINE COMMUNITIES

ANIKA GUPTA

TILLER PRESS

New York   London   Toronto   Sydney   New Delhi

An Imprint of Simon & Schuster, Inc.
1230 Avenue of the Americas
New York, NY 10020

First Tiller Press trade paperback edition August 2020

TILLER PRESS and colophon are trademarks of Simon & Schuster, Inc.

For information about special discounts for bulk purchases,
please contact Simon & Schuster Special Sales at 1-866-506-1949
or business@simonandschuster.com.

The Simon & Schuster Speakers Bureau can bring authors to your live event.
For more information or to book an event, contact the Simon & Schuster Speakers
Bureau at 1-866-248-3049 or visit our website at www.simonspeakers.com.

Interior design by Laura Levatino

Manufactured in the United States of America

1 3 5 7 9 10 8 6 4 2

Library of Congress Cataloging-in-Publication Data has been applied for.

ISBN 978-1-9821-3231-6
ISBN 978-1-9821-3232-3 (ebook)

For my family

Contents

Introduction

Why Moderators Matter

Some of our earliest communities were bounded and defined by geography. In 2005, when the academic researchers Jenny Preece and Diane Maloney-Krichmar wrote an essay about online communities for the *Journal of Computer-Mediated Communication*, they began by saying, "Until the advent of telecommunications technology, definitions of community focused on close-knit groups in a single location. Factors such as birth and physical location determined belonging to a community."[1] But then communications networks expanded. As the internet and then social media came into existence, the boundaries of the modern community expanded beyond what people in those early communities might have imagined. We began to spend time in online groups. These groups weren't defined only by geography, religion, or birth; they included an expanding array of ever-more-niche interests. In researching this book, I came across online groups dedicated to all of the following: a specific cooking implement; a particular and now-discontinued science fiction show; home-brewed cosmetics; and the word "yikes." Joining an online community today is an act of self-definition, even when it's something as simple as clicking the "Join" button on a Facebook page or the "Subscribe" button on a YouTube profile.

As with geographic communities, even a simple online community can require enormous work to sustain. Who defines the boundaries and identities of the community? Who makes and enforces rules? In the geographic community, there were "authorities"—elders, leaders, officials. Online, those roles are performed by many different individuals and agencies: participants, software companies, governments. In their essay, Preece and Maloney-Krichmar eventually settle on the following definition for an online community: "the *people* who come together for a particular *purpose*, and who are guided by *policies* (including norms and rules) and supported by *software*."[2]

People, purpose, policies, software. Powerful technology companies like Facebook and Google build the software, then draft terms and conditions that specify how people can use their tools. They have enormous power to decide who connects with whom, and how. Governments also play a role—they specify legal consequences for certain types of online behavior. They can ban pornography, gambling, and prostitution on the internet, for example, and companies and individuals will have to comply.

But technology alone isn't enough. In a study of online groups, the researchers Brian Butler, Lee Sproull, Sara Kiesler, and Robert Kraut explain the "social behavior" required:

> First, people must tend the tools themselves by managing software versions, keeping address files up to date, and so on. People also must recruit members to replace

those who leave. They must manage social dynamics. They must participate. Without these group maintenance activities, even sophisticated tools and infrastructure will not sustain viable online groups.[3]

The people in a group create purpose and policies among themselves. They work with software, but also around and through it. For example, Twitter provides a platform where people can send short messages out into the world. In theory, these messages can be only 280 characters long, but people build linked tweets into chains or "threads." There are whole online conventions around how to label a Twitter thread so that it becomes a sequential argument. The author Jennifer Egan wrote an entire short story in tweets, subverting the medium's brevity. People do fascinating things to get around and through the restrictions and limitations of the software they use, sometimes transforming its original or intended purpose in order to better suit a social need.

Participants also craft policies. Many online communities these days have additional policies beyond the terms and conditions required by the platform. These policies appear in a variety of places: in sidebars on forums, in questions that people have to answer before they join the community, in introductory or pinned posts at the top of a message board. In addition to written rules, communities often have unwritten rules and codes of behavior, developed among members over time. These norms are powerful, too—they can influence who feels welcome in the community, how members post, and how other people respond. Where do these policies come from? How are they enforced? It turns out that this work doesn't fall on everyone equally. There are some people who do more of the work in online communities than others. They're called moderators.

The Rise of the Moderator

"Moderator" is a new-ish job title. According to more traditional definitions, it's barely a job title at all. Many moderators work for free, volunteering many hours every week to update their community's technology, manage relationships, and recruit and train other moderators. The skills the job requires are as old as human conversation and overlap with those needed for customer service, digital media, marketing, conflict mediation, and event management. Moderating draws on the tradition of the bard or the storyteller, as well as the host.

Of course, moderation work isn't limited to volunteers. As more and more people join and share ideas in social networks, organizations, governments, and brands operate in these spaces also. Paid customer-service specialists and community liaisons often do moderation work. So do audience development editors and some journalists. Many "influencers" either manage their own communities or recruit other people to do it.

How to Handle a Crowd deals mainly with volunteer moderators (although there are two exceptions: someone who started out as a volunteer moderator and then was hired for the role, and a YouTube influencer who went full-time). These moderators have certain responsibilities in common: they add or remove users, write rules and guidelines, message people one-on-one to talk about rules violations, approve posts, and intervene in online arguments.

Through careful and constant work, moderators also shape their communities in the long term, and this is perhaps the most important function they perform. When they draft rules and admit or remove people, moderators shape not only the community's structure but also its fundamental identity. In this task, they sometimes receive support from the companies whose software they use; social media companies realize that they depend on moderators to keep communities healthy and to keep users coming back. Representatives at platforms like Facebook, YouTube, and Reddit regularly reach out to moderators of large groups. They offer them invitations to moderator-only groups and events, offer them the chance to give early feedback on new features, and give them priority access to tech support. Platforms also offer moderators access to information that other members of the community might not have, in order to help them moderate better: historical records of individual users' behavior, special communication channels for moderators only, and graphs or charts of things like comments and interactions over time.

Considering how much power moderators can have over the online experience, why don't we know more about the job itself? Possibly because not that many people choose to become moderators, because it can feel like a thankless task. One of the key questions that Butler and his colleagues asked in their study was why moderators put in all that work. When writing this book, I asked that same question. I talked to moderators from many different kinds of communities. I learned how they did their jobs, how they negotiated with technology companies, and how they handled the inevitable drama that arises whenever groups of humans interact with one another. They also told me about the "dark side" of moderation—what makes it difficult, and how they handle some of the unique challenges online culture has enabled.

While academics might debate what constitutes an online "community," many moderators have a clear sense of the goals they're working toward, and for whom. Here's one response from a moderator I spoke to, when asked how she defines an online community:

> It doesn't have to be big, and it doesn't have to be one homogenous thing. . . . Some people connect with each other more than others, and that's okay. But the fact that everyone shows up and stays in the room [means] we have a pretty engaged group. The desire to support each other in difficult times and on difficult topics is how I see community.

Here's another definition, from the cofounder of an online activist movement:

> I think it's a shared set of values and principles, and a shared mission and ethics, and also just the ability to communicate with each other and share ideas, and that's what makes any community.

And there's this one, from the founder and operator of a twenty-year-old email LISTSERV for a (geographically!) small neighborhood in Washington, DC:

I'm willing to accept if you live kind of within an area that anybody would call Cleveland Park and you care about the community, you're a Cleveland Parker.

These moderators have a vision for what they want their communities to be: places of shared purpose, support, or care. It's possible that some people are drawn to setting up online communities *because* they value these aspects of social relationships. In their study, Butler and his colleagues found that "people who valued social benefits reported performing more community building work of all types."[4] Is the impulse to build and maintain an online community the same one that, in years past, might have led someone to bring soup to a sick neighbor or to host a dinner party? The founders of at least one community I study in this book make that link pretty explicitly. While it's not the only motivation that came up, it did come up repeatedly.

Each of the chapters that follows is its own profile. You can read them all at once, or just the ones you're most interested in. Each of the moderators—and in some cases, moderation teams—whom I profile are working toward a different goal, even though similar themes and challenges emerge in all their work.

The first chapter describes a movement called "Make America Dinner Again" (MADA for short). The moderators of MADA started out hosting in-person dinners for people with different political views. MADA's goal was to use tasty food and guided conversation to bridge partisan political divides. Eventually the two founding moderators started an accompanying Facebook group, and today that seven-hundred-member group includes people from all across the American political spectrum. The participants regularly debate topics like abortion, secularism, and gun rights, among the thorniest issues in public discourse.

Chapter two continues to delve into difficult conversations by tackling the internet's third rail—race—through the eyes of the moderators of two very different groups. The first group I profile is Pantsuit Nation, which claims to be one of the largest groups on Facebook. The group includes about three million members, and was formed to support Hillary Clinton in the 2016 presidential election. After the election, moderators faced critiques from within the group about how they handled topics of race. They've tried to adapt to these challenges, including hiring a director of engagement to address them. Then there's Real Talk: WOC & Allies for Racial Justice and Anti-Oppression. Initially born out of the founders' frustration with Pantsuit Nation, Real Talk has grown into its own powerful ecosystem. The moderators have created anti-racism online training modules for members and adapted Facebook's platform to parcel their group into separate "rooms" for different types of conversation.

Chapter three looks into local moderation: the people who link together our neighborhoods. I interview moderators of neighborhood groups and LISTSERVs about how they forge civic purpose and prevent discord among neighbors. One of these groups was in the midst of transitioning platforms when I spoke to them. The story of their shift illustrates how online communities adapt to change, and the key role that moderators play in resilience. This chapter also includes an interview with the founder and local chapter leader of NUMTOT, an urbanism-focused online group that's become famous for its size and its ability to attract younger people to Facebook. Finally, the chapter concludes with the story of the Sacramento Sister Circle, an online community for Black women in Sacramento, California. The members of Sister Circle have used the group to discover common purpose and organize offline political action.

No book about online groups would be complete without at least one chapter on online activism. Chapter four tells the story of Sleeping Giants, an online movement that's used Twitter and Facebook to pressure brands into withdrawing advertising from right-leaning media organizations. The founders have taken a complex and timely subject—online advertising—and turned it into a rallying cry for a disaffected liberal generation, inspiring chapters in many other countries along the way. Sleeping Giants' founders were initially anonymous, until one of them was doxxed, meaning his identity was revealed without his consent. The other founder then chose to reveal her identity. Their story demonstrates the dark side of mass online action, but also its potential influence and power in a time when brands can lose customers and face over a poorly worded tweet.

Chapter five heads in an entirely different direction. I ride along with groups that play massively multiplayer online games together, learning about how these groups form and what keeps them going. I profile two very different group leaders, each with a specific philosophy toward their game. Online gaming may feel like the pinnacle of fantasy, but the relationships people form in these games have profound implications for offline identity. These groups also use a variety of platforms and interfaces to conduct conversations, define roles, and organize action.

Chapter six follows the founder and lead moderator of a popular message board on the community site Reddit. Reddit is one of the most-visited sites on the internet, and its many communities are led by a cadre of powerful—and sometimes controversial—volunteer moderators. The moderator talks about how he's built on Reddit's existing tools, how his team invites applications for new moderators, and how they prepare for what he describes as "constant Eternal September"—an ongoing influx of new members that, if left unmanaged, could overrun the forum and destroy its culture. Reddit is a busy universe, and this particular moderation team works constantly to sustain and manage their global community.

Chapter seven introduces an aspiring novelist who turned to making YouTube videos partly because he felt that traditional publishing was broken. He set up a membership program on the creator-focused site Patreon and has slowly but steadily grown a niche community of horror-video enthusiasts. He wrestles with how to manage YouTube's copyright protections, as well as how to manage community on a variety of different platforms. Along the way, he reflects on what it means to be a private figure in a public space, and how he's grown his "horror host" personality online.

The final chapter is about FetLife, an online social network dedicated to kink. Millions of people use FetLife to research a mind-boggling array of fetishes, post pictures and profiles, and—of course—find people to hook up with. I interview one of the moderators of the site's largest groups, Novices & Newbies. This newcomer-focused group serves many functions: welcome lobby, training ground, camp orientation. The lead moderator has been running the group for years, adapting FetLife's tools to his own purposes. FetLife moderators also have to contend with regulations around adult content online, the changing nature of which has caused significant challenges for the site as a whole. The interplay between group and community guidelines reflects the fine balance of power among moderators, the audiences they serve, and the platforms that host their communities. It also demonstrates the far-reaching impacts of government regulation of online behavior.

I wrote this book before the global coronavirus pandemic irrevocably changed how we think about online communities. Around the world, millions of people were told to stay home, and online gatherings became our only way to stay connected. The pandemic makes this book possibly even more useful than before, although it also raises a lot of questions. Will neighbors, who used local LISTSERVs to help each other during the pandemic, stay friends after it ends? Will an ever-greater percentage of the world's workforce, suddenly forced to work from home, continue doing so indefinitely? Will conferences move online permanently? What does all this mean for equity, access, and online moderators? Hopefully this book helps the many more people who've suddenly found themselves moderating, while also pointing out a potential path forward as we try to discover a new normal in a much more connected world.

How Did I Find and Choose People to Interview?

Although there's no single definition of an online community, I considered the following things to be significant when deciding whom to interview.

1. Is the communication within the community many-to-many? A one-to-one conversation is, of course, a dialogue. A one-to-many conversation is a television broadcast or a newspaper article. But I was interested in how moderators shaped or influenced conversations and identity among groups of people, and most inter-ested in groups in which lots of people were talking to one another at once. A Facebook group in which people interact frequently and constantly with a variety of others in the group qualifies. A YouTube comments section doesn't necessarily qualify, unless it has a regular base of people who communicate with each other and not just with the video's creator. This doesn't mean that YouTube creators don't have communities—in fact, I profile one—but rather that they're keeping in touch via many different mechanisms.

2. Are relationships being built and maintained online? Is the online component significant in terms of how the group defines itself? Many of these communities have offline components—NUMTOT has spawned local spin-off chapters that meet in person, and MADA started as an actual dinner series. But for the purposes of this book, I wanted communities where moderators were invested in—and had to put energy into—the community's online component. In other words, a sporadic Facebook conversation among a group of in-person friends, while interesting, didn't

qualify. A Reddit forum where people don't know one another in person but are creating conversations, identities, and relationships online, does.

3. Does the group have a moderator or leader, whether de facto or defined? Do *other* people in the community recognize that the moderator has special power to shape the conversation, admit members, or take on responsibilities that other community members don't? This is a tougher question than it seems, since moderation in online groups exists on many levels. Platforms moderate when they create guidelines or hire people to filter out objectionable content, and people moderate when they set guidelines or create rules. Prior to the revelation of the founders' identities, for example, the Sleeping Giants Twitter and Facebook communities felt like a collective. But the entire group recognized that the main handle was driving the agenda and responding to people, so the people who ran that handle qualified as moderators.

One of the challenges in understanding moderation work is that the term "moderator" is both informative and misleading. Many moderators talk about managing conflict and extremity—keeping things moderate, in a literal sense. The most visible signs of moderation are actions like removing posts or banning users, which can lead to the misconception that this type of public work is all that moderators do. Claudia Lo, a researcher and Reddit moderator who has studied online moderation, called the popular perception of online moderation the "reactive" model, and notes that it has severe limitations: "By tying all moderator work to direct reactions, short-term moderator action is disproportionately emphasized, while longer-term moderation work tends to be overlooked."[5]

Claudia opened her study with a personal example: One evening, a user posted a question on a forum she moderates. She got a notification about the post on her phone. She negotiated a new policy on the fly that night, and the next day, she and several fellow moderators privately talked about that policy and what it might mean for their forum's users. In the end, they decided they didn't need to ban anyone from the forum or remove any content. She said, "Nothing was removed, so by the popular standards of online moderation, *no moderation had happened.*"[6] But she contends that she was doing longer-term work: negotiating the boundaries of a conversation and setting purpose, direction, and pace. *How to Handle a Crowd* is about both short-term moderation work—how and when to ban a user or a comment—and the longer-term side of moderation. When the founders of MADA get together and talk about the balance of political viewpoints they want in their group, they're doing longer-term community work, as are the moderators of Real Talk when they debate which homework assignments they should offer in their anti-racism training or Reddit moderators when they talk about preparing for Eternal September. These types of work often flow into each other. Deciding what mix of political viewpoints to include in the MADA group informs whom the moderators admit and how they respond to those members' individual comments. Longer-term moderation work enables short-term work; it doesn't exclude it.

Many of the moderators I interviewed for this book are volunteers. For volunteers, moderation requires not just judgment and negotiation skills but extreme comfort with multitasking. One moderator told me about frantically moderating an exploding Facebook discussion in the moments before a friend's wedding ceremony in Scotland. He took a break during the ceremony, and then checked in again afterward to make sure the discussion had calmed down. One moderator explained to me how she and her moderation team have learned to "read" Facebook notifications: whenever they receive a series of notifications that the same users are posting repeatedly, it's likely that a disagreement is in the works. One moderator told me, possibly ruefully, "We don't get weekends off." He'd been running online communities in one capacity or another for more than ten years.

Although many teams designate when a moderator is "on," it's a lot harder to define exactly when a moderator is "off," especially because moderation spaces tend to overlap with personal interests. One former volunteer moderator told me she often felt constantly responsible for the communities she used to manage, hesitating to put down her phone. Another moderator told me he often experiences "compassion fatigue," a sense of emotional exhaustion born of constantly thinking about and working to understand the many personalities in his group. Some fantasize about switching their communities off entirely. Moderator burnout is a real and frequent event. Moderation teams turn over, and the moderators in this book often think about how to blow off steam or provide space for their teams to relax.

The moderator role is also contested. It's where the conflict between individual volunteers, paid platform employees, and platform policies coalesces. This is directly the result of companies' business models, according to a 2015 *New York Times Magazine* article by veteran technology journalist Adrian Chen:

> The hottest tech companies no longer want to run communities, with all their messy, unprofitable human drama. Instead, they want to make platforms: slick, frictionless, infinitely monetizable. Companies like Facebook and Google try to create the illusion that their platforms are moderated by algorithms, not people.[7]

In the years since Chen wrote that article, films like *The Cleaners*, as well as a series of investigative articles, have revealed that Facebook employs an army of low-paid contract workers who mine Facebook's problematic posts. These contractors watch the posts that other users have flagged as offensive; their job is to remove anything that contains extremely violent or illegal content. They spend long hours viewing things as horrid as stabbings and animal abuse. These employees have later said that they experienced secondary traumatic stress—similar in its symptoms to post-traumatic stress disorder—after constant exposure to so much gruesome content.[8]

There is overlap between the work that community and contract moderators do, but the structural positions they enjoy within their communities are different. In this book, I focus on people I refer to as community moderators. I define community moderation work as visibly building relationships and community identity over time. The community moderators I interview are therefore known to the other members of their communities and enmeshed in the complex webs of relationships that comprise the communities' cores. Contracted moderators operating on behalf of tech companies are barred from participating in these relationships; most members and users of the platforms will never know these contractors' names. There are full-time, paid employees who perform moderation and community management work on behalf of platforms. Some of these employees occupy a liminal space between community and content moderation. They operate at the platform level but can be named and shamed by individual community members, and their identities certainly come into play during disputes. This is what happened in early 2019 when community members accused several paid administrators of the community site Discord of favoring "furries" in their terms of service.[9] (It should be noted that Discord, despite its rapidly expanding userbase, which we talk about more in later chapters, is a relatively new service, so their moderation work will possibly be more in flux.)

Although these different forms of moderation overlap, the ways in which they influence a community, and the ways in which other members recognize that influence, are very different.

A Note on Methods, Quotes, and Anonymity

My interest in online communities goes back many years. From 2014 to 2016, for my graduate thesis, I spent two years interviewing people who managed online comment sections, mainly at news organizations. The people I met were caught at many crossroads: between the ethics of traditional journalism, which valued journalistic expertise, and the emerging values of the participatory internet, which valued transparency; between the desire to create thriving community spaces and the corporate pressure to deliver monetizable pageviews; between their professional passion for the subjects they moderated and their personal exhaustion with trolling and attacks; between the civic goals of journalism and a total lack of platform or managerial support to improve the experience on their sites. They introduced me to ideas that would later come to form the heart of this book, too: conflicts over payment versus volunteerism, community care and emotional work, and what role platforms can or should play in helping moderators do their jobs. I benefited from having done this prior research, and so, where it makes sense, I've included references to that prior work in this text.

Comment sections—especially on news websites—rarely lived up to their promise in terms of civil dialogue, and even when they did, it didn't always last long. But the central questions of what constitutes an online community and what it takes to create successful ones remain as fascinating and important as ever.

In addition to the criteria mentioned earlier in this introduction, when it came time to find potential interviewees for this book, I put out a call on—appropriately—social media. I asked friends to refer me to people they knew, and that brought me into contact with several of the people I've profiled. I also read articles and research papers and reached out via direct messages on social media sites. If you're looking for a statistically representative sample of online communities, you won't find that here. That kind of sample is probably impossible, given the varying definitions of the term "online community." Instead, I've tried to include a sample of different types of communities and different platforms. This sample wound up being weighted a little more toward Facebook than I would have initially liked. I also wish I'd written about the globally popular and deeply influential messaging platform WhatsApp, or Instagram. Perhaps next time. There's never enough time to get to everything, and every moderator in this book has something fascinating to say about their work.

These moderators spent several hours talking to me. I'm profoundly grateful to them; these conversations were the greatest pleasure of writing this book. My interviewees introduced me to worlds I would never have entered otherwise. I hope their stories do the same for you.

Some of the people I interviewed asked to be identified by their legal names, while others preferred the aliases that they use online. In every case, I let interviewees choose how to be identified. When someone uses an alias, I make note of it. I spent several hours in every community I profile in this book, with a few exceptions. One is the Sacramento Sister Circle. It's a community exclusively for Black women, and the moderator felt it would be inappropriate for me to join. Instead, I looked up reports on the Sister Circle in local media, and used those reports to verify some of the events that the moderator, Christi, describes. The other exceptions are two of the Final Fantasy free companies that appear in the chapter about MMORPGs; these are primarily open only to friends and family.

I also came up with an approach to quoting people. I quote

directly from my interviews, and from comments that my moderators and interviewees have posted online. When dealing with closed communities—those that require an invitation to join—I never directly quoted a comment unless I had permission from the person who posted it, although I did sometimes summarize discussions in more general terms. I quoted comments that were visible via public web search—YouTube comments, for example—but tried to stick to general comments that expressed the overall zeitgeist. I directly quote publicly visible articles and blog posts. There are no clear lines here, but wherever possible, I also tried to provide context for the comments I've included.

If you're at all interested in the question of how we communicate and form groups, or how we negotiate identity and award authority in our expanding online universe, then this book is for you. If you're a media professional who works in digital communications, you'll find many examples of how other moderators handle challenging situations, as well as how they wrestle with the interpersonal and identity issues that arise as a result of that work. If you study human-computer interaction, you'll discover yet another perspective on how human relationships and behavior shape our uses of extremely popular technology. If you're a volunteer moderator, then hopefully you'll see this book as a tribute to what you already do well and a guide to new ideas that can improve your work. And if you're a commenter on the internet, like I am, hopefully you'll gain some insight into what happens to your comment after you click "publish"—as well as what had to happen in order for you to be able to click "publish" in the first place.

HOW TO HANDLE A CROWD

1.

Building Bridges

Make America Dinner Again

How I Met MADA

I met Justine Lee for the first time in New York. We'd "met" online months before, while working together on a podcast project about Asian American life. I asked her for suggestions for whom to profile in this book; she recommended herself. Over a couple of hours, Justine told me her story. Since October 2017, she and her friend Tria Chang have run a Facebook group called Make America Dinner Again (MADA). The name pokes fun at partisan rhetoric, but the group has a serious purpose: to encourage understanding and dialogue among people with differing political views. Justine and Tria started the group after the 2016 presidential election, and it now has almost seven hundred members. Those who want to join have to apply by answering a few questions on Facebook; the founders read each application thoroughly and personally. As MADA has grown, they've accepted new members with an eye toward political balance; Justine says the group today includes roughly equal numbers of self-identified liberals and conservatives, as well as many other perspectives. The two of them, along with nine other moderators, oversee debates about the most divisive political topics in American discourse. Recent posts include one comparing restrictions on gun ownership to restrictions on book ownership, another asking whether or not a Holocaust-denying school principal should have been fired, and a third asking how San Francisco can humanely resolve escalating rates of homelessness.

Their group is part of a growing movement, born in the run-up to and wake of the 2016 presidential election, focused on building bridges across what seems to be an ever-widening political divide. In any given week, the MADA moderators research and post articles for the wider group to discuss, contact group members one-on-one to offer advice on the tone or content of their posts, or—in Justine's case—read through short surveys filled out by people who want to join the group. But their real work is trying to shore up common ideals in a divided world, building slim but strong bridges across the divide of partisan opinion. Justine refers to this type of work as "translating." The group is sometimes fractious, sometimes hopeful, and often challenging. But in working there, Justine and Tria have established an interesting online home.

The Lost Art of the Dinner Party

MADA grew out of Justine and Tria's feelings about the 2016 election. A self-described political liberal living in San Francisco, Justine says she woke up in a daze the day after Donald J. Trump was elected president. She didn't know how to respond. She wasn't alone: liberals across the country were torn and dismayed. In a popular blog post written right after the election, political science professor Peter Levine outlined several potential responses that the left could make. These possible responses included things like "winning the next election," "resisting the administration," and "reforming politics." They also included "repairing the civic fabric" via "dialog across partisan divides."[1] This last category is the one that Justine and Tria would come to belong to.

Justine had just finished a public radio internship, which had exposed her to local politics. But she'd found politics to be "inaccessible and a little overwhelming." Instead she enjoyed the "human stories," in part because "I've always believed that there are multiple sides to a story." That curiosity about other people, and a focus on the human face of political debates, would become the core principles of MADA.

"Dialog across partisan divides" sounds great in theory, but is difficult in practice. In a June 2016 study by the Pew Research Center, nearly half of self-identified Republicans and Democrats said they found discussing politics with someone with opposing political views to be "stressful and frustrating," and more than half said that they left such conversations feeling like they had less in common than they originally thought.[2] Maybe just as troubling, at least from a national unity perspective, was that Republicans and Democrats saw each other in a *personally* poor light, ascribing negative qualities like laziness or closed-mindedness to those on the other side of the political divide.[3] Researchers refer to this type of partisan dislike as "affective polarization." In a seminal

2012 paper, the researchers Shanto Iyengar, Gaurav Sood, and Yphtach Lelkes demonstrated that affective polarization in the United States had risen dramatically since 1988, as measured by things like whether or not people would be upset if their child married someone from a different political party. In another paper, published in 2019, a group of researchers suggested that affective polarization could have serious consequences: "Partisanship appears to now compromise the norms and standards we apply to our elected representatives, and even leads partisans to call into question the legitimacy of election results, both of which threaten the very foundations of representative democracy."[4]

In the months before the election, Justine says she saw political conversations break down, time and again, in her own social media feeds. People often talked past each other.

"Anytime there was a news article posted on our FB feeds, we would see it in the comments. People would make a statement in response to the headline. They would come out really strong, with almost no room for dialogue." The worst, she says, were the comment sections on news organizations like Fox News or CNN, which she says turned into a "a mass of name-calling and trolling and inflammatory language."

Platforms like Facebook had enormous reach and scale, but neither their technology nor their business models prioritized the facilitation of wide-ranging conversations. On the contrary, algorithms that powered popular social media sites often encouraged like-minded bubbles. A popular *Wall Street Journal* project from the time, called Blue Feed, Red Feed, compared how liberal and conservative Facebook news feeds featured different stories, from different outlets, with different slants.[5] "If you wanted to widen your perspective and see things from a broad range of backgrounds, you would have to go and like the pages yourself. Facebook's product makes it hard to do this," Jon Keegan, the project's creator, told media industry site NiemanLab in May 2016.[6]

But there was a flip side to the name-calling: entirely homogeneous spaces where people never interacted with anyone who had opposing views.

"If it was something that was posted on our friends' feeds . . . everyone was in agreement, but it almost felt narrower still," Justine said.

She recruited her friend Tria Chang, a wedding planner who also lived in San Francisco, to host a dinner party for people with opposing political views. Their hope was that under the auspices of a shared meal, Democrats and Republicans might discover even more common ground.

Tria already had experience with unusually tense events—weddings, she says, "are more complex than people" imagine. A lot of the tension at weddings lives beneath the surface—in part because people repress the "negative but natural emotions" that they might have about, say, a friend getting married and leaving them behind, or a child embarking on a new and independent life stage. A party among people with different political views can feel the same way: barely comfortable, and then only if people skirt the issues they really care about. Justine and Tria wanted to bring these sources of tension to the surface, and in talking about them, try to make people more comfortable with hard conversations. Doing it within the safe and familiar ritual of dinnertime would, they hoped, make participants feel more secure.

"We're sharing a meal together, there's already this understanding that we're all coming with good intentions," said Justine about the choice.

The dinner party carries a lot of weight as a symbol and stand-in for social life. In the bestselling 2000 book *Bowling Alone: The Collapse and Revival of American Community*, political scientist Robert D. Putnam traces several contributing factors in the decline of American civic engagement over the past several decades. He spends a lot of time talking about the dinner party, noting that "Americans are spending a lot less time breaking bread with friends than we did twenty or thirty years ago."[7] In the ancient world, it was a deep and unpardonable offense to break bread with someone and then betray that hospitality, either in word or deed. Texts from the *Odyssey* to the Bible describe the dreadful character of—and dire consequences for—ungrateful guests. The ritual of dinner runs deep in our blood, certainly deeper than partisan divides. "Food can act as a conversation starter, but also as a buffer, in some way. If there's nothing to talk about, if it's awkward or uncomfortable, you can talk about the food in front of you," Justine said. She grew up cooking with her family, while Tria organized dinner parties for a living. They liked the in-person element of a dinner, characterized by long and deep discussion—the opposite of the impersonal, quick-take attack culture they saw online.

If the idea of a brief conversation with a political opponent raises most people's hackles, a structured three-hour dinner probably sounds like torture. Justine and Tria's initial idea attracted resistance from both conservatives and liberals, Justine says. Activist friends preferred to focus on direct action in response to the election. The two of them knew very few conservatives, so they took out Facebook ads to try to recruit some. The ads, featuring what they thought was an appealing photo and a fun message, backfired. Conservatives—the minority in deeply liberal San Francisco—feared that the dinner invitation might be a ploy to expose or humiliate them. They also had no idea who Justine and Tria were—after all, relationships are built on trust, and Justine and Tria had yet to build any among San Francisco's conservative population.

The women soon realized that one of the first things they would have to do was "humanize" the people on the other side of the voting divide, including to themselves. After the election, Tria says she was briefly afraid to leave the house. She associated Trump with sexism and racism, and as a woman of color, she says she felt personally targeted by all the votes that had been cast for Trump. She "felt this fear brewing in me, and I know that fear can quickly turn to hate and I didn't want to be walking around filled with hate because that would be . . . unhealthy for . . . my community." In order to build bridges, Tria had to step away from that sense of fear, toward a sense of optimism and openness. They eventually recruited some conservative guests through their wider social network instead. They asked each potential participant to answer a few brief questions in order to get a sense of their goals and discussion style. As the day for their first dinner party neared, they began to think about how they, as the facilitators, could help their guests reach this same attitude of openness and optimism.

They also attended to logistics. Pizza felt like a familiar and neutral food choice, and they chose a restaurant in downtown San Francisco that was easily accessible via transit. On a drizzly weeknight in January, they opened the doors. When attendees made their way to the restaurant's private room, they found special printed menus waiting for them, as well as dice and kazoos laid out on the tables.

The dice were part of an introductory game. Each side of a die corresponded to a question that attendees could ask each other. Questions included things like "Who in your life has influenced you the most?" and, appropriately for the venue, "Given the choice of anyone in the world, who would you want as a dinner guest?" The kazoos were to keep things comfortable: if guests needed a moderator to intervene in the discussion, they could toot the kazoo to get Justine or Tria's attention.

Justine and Tria planned the evening down to the minute, even going so far as to write out instructions and dialogue for themselves in a detailed "run of show" document. The first part of the dinner, right after people arrived, was a time for "softball questions," things like "Where are you from?" and "What made you interested in coming to dinner tonight?" Justine and Tria wrote down the following advice for themselves, the moderators:

Give each speaker our totally absorbed and undivided attention and empathy, whatever they're saying. Some "heavy talkers" will need to be interrupted. Some more shy folks will need to be drawn out. That's our main job, to ensure that a diverse range of speakers are heard and to perhaps offer a comment or insight here or there.

The document offers a clear perspective on both their strategy and their priorities: for example, they rank communication and listening above changing people's minds. (In fact, the idea of changing people's minds doesn't appear as a goal anywhere in the document, or really, in their moderation philosophy.)

After the softball questions, the group paired off to get to know each other better. They talked about whom they'd voted for in the recent election and why. Afterward, for the final half hour of the dinner, the group came together to discuss more sensitive matters. Justine and Tria wrote down questions like:

- How do you feel about large-scale protests like the Women's March on Washington, set to occur after the inauguration? Do you think they are useful; if so, what do you think they can or will accomplish?
- How do you feel about the likely congressional repeal of the ACA? Will it affect you personally in any way? If so, how?

At the end of the dinner, the moderators passed around sticky notes. People wrote down their hopes and dreams for the country. They put their sticky notes up on a wall, and found points of similarity and difference.

The group ended up discussing only three of the scripted questions. Once lubricated with drinks and food, guests found their own rhythm and the conversation never lagged. At the end, when it came time to share hopes and dreams, the group found several points of commonality, including a dislike for the way the media had covered the most recent election, and a hope for more support for the middle class under the new president.

Reducing partisan distrust is difficult because it's hard to pinpoint what exactly causes this type of distrust, and also because political identity is complex and interacts with many other aspects of self. Nonetheless, research has suggested that focusing on similarities instead of differences—like Justine and Tria did with their Post-it Note exercise—can help.[8] Both liberals and conservatives tend to overestimate the extremity of other people's political views, even within their own party, so gatherings that bring together those with more moderate views could help counteract that bias.[9]

Justine and Tria went home exhausted, but also hopeful. Justine felt that the evening provided a powerful counter-response to their critics. It was "just a . . . gathering at the end of the day," she acknowledged, but "it is possible."

They didn't plan to repeat the dinner for several months. But a journalist who attended the first dinner wrote a story that ran on National Public Radio. Production companies and journalists reached out to Justine and Tria to organize more dinners, and they got emails from interested participants and hosts all over the country. What began as a one-off dinner grew into a series, and eventually into a network, with chapters in several major cities, each chapter headed by a local organizer. But their concept remained emphatically in-person, among co-located participants, until later in 2017.

The Opposite of the Comments Section

It's not hard to find examples of online political discussions run amok. When Lisa Conn joined Facebook as an employee in the summer of 2017, she wanted to find examples of the opposite: online political discussions that had helped people learn and find common ground. Before joining Facebook, she was a product manager at the MIT Media Lab and worked on a project that tracked how people talked about politics, elections, and policy on Twitter. Like others doing similar work around the country, she and her colleagues found that social media—in theory, a powerful tool for creating community—could also create closed networks of conversation among like-minded people. "Giving the world power to build communities doesn't necessarily bring the world closer together," she said. "Building communities can actually tear the world apart, by limiting people's contact with those who have opposing views."

It was a finding that Facebook's leadership had begun to appreciate as well, as they tried to figure out the role that Facebook should play in society. The company had started to receive complaints that its platform and algorithms didn't do enough to protect users' privacy or halt the spread of misinformation. News reports had surfaced that Cambridge Analytica, an election data firm based in the UK, had accessed millions of

Facebook users' personal data without consent, and used this information to help conservative politicians get elected.[10] All of these things presented serious challenges for Facebook's platform and philosophy. In 2017, the company changed its mission statement from "Making the world more open and connected" to "Give people the power to build community and bring the world closer together," a shift toward actively promoting cohesion.[11] In a video interview with CNN Tech, Facebook CEO Mark Zuckerberg described the company's new mission: "Our society is still very divided, and that means that people need to work proactively to help bring people closer together."[12]

Lisa, who proudly says her grandmother was a civil rights activist, wanted to know if, through active and thoughtful moderation, online spaces could be made to do the opposite of what her research team had observed at MIT. Could online discussions encourage dialogue among people with diverging views? Despite what she describes as a lack of popular trust in the Facebook brand at the time, she was "genuinely concerned about the ways in which extremism and polarization were flourishing in social media." Her goal was to identify possible improvements to Facebook's Groups feature, by learning from people who were bridging gaps and fighting polarization. Soon after she started at Facebook, she met Justine and Tria through a colleague.

At the time, MADA was still an in-person group. The three of them talked about whether there could be a way to extend the MADA philosophy into a Facebook group format. Justine and Tria had hesitations. After all, they'd formed MADA as a counter-response to the impersonal, attack-driven culture they saw in their own social media feeds. Many of the dinner's focal moments involved participants looking into one another's eyes and responding to one another in real time. These types of conversations give people plenty of chances to observe what researchers refer to as "symbolic cues"—a wink, a shrug, a sigh—that can be just as telling as their actual words.[13] Justine and Tria considered the act of paying attention to others' symbolic cues part of the "humanization" process. That level of context gets lost online, when people don't always know each other's real names, don't see nonverbal cues, and can enter and leave conversations without notice.

But an online group offered benefits, too—including scale, reach, and potential longevity. Justine and Tria were already facing challenges as MADA grew. The first was geography—they didn't have enough hosts to meet demand, especially in less densely populated areas. Second, they wanted to capture the energy and enthusiasm that participants felt after a dinner by giving them a place to keep the conversation going, but that wasn't always an option in physical space.

They perceived other benefits, also. There are plenty of people for whom an in-person dinner is not accessible, because of temperament, ability, or other reasons, but an online group might be. Among online platforms, Facebook had enormous scale and ubiquity, as well as tools for groups that would, in theory, give moderators greater control and agency in guiding conversation. With careful, thoughtful, and diligent moderation, perhaps an online version of MADA could help keep the spirit of the project alive.

They gave the same careful treatment to their online moderation practices that they had to their offline moderation. Several weeks before launching the Facebook group, Justine, Tria, and Lisa drew up a three-column spreadsheet identifying eleven top-level MADA "goals." These included things like "give people the agency to ask for help," "show that people's views are complex," and "connect people 1:1 after the dinner." In the next column of the spreadsheet, they listed how MADA achieved each of these goals through in-person moderation practices. For example, at an in-person dinner, participants got noisemakers—like the ka-zoos from the first dinner—or a set of red and green cards that they could hold up to show the moderators that they needed help or felt uncomfortable.

In the third column, the three brainstormed ways to achieve these same goals in the Facebook group. For example, they pro-posed "green/yellow/red emoji" and a "bell emoji" as ways par-ticipants could indicate discomfort or get moderators' attention. To help people show a variety of views, they suggested "create a poll with multiple answers," and to build one-to-one connections, they considered "encourage friending."

They built the group slowly over time, trying to maintain a balance of political perspectives. Just like the in-person dinners, they asked everyone who wanted to join to answer a few initial questions. In reviewing hopeful participants' answers, Justine often also looked at the person's public Facebook profile to get a sense of how they expressed themselves online.

Some of these ideas worked better than others. The bell emoji, for example, never quite took off. Instead, Justine says, they noticed that other members of the group started stepping into heated discussions to remind participants of the rules. As the group expanded, Justine and Tria began to approach some of these extra-helpful members as potential moderators. This is one way to expand a moderation team—by offering additional responsibility to people who are already informally taking on work.

Mark Fosdal was one of those people. He's in his fifties, grew up in the Midwest, and describes himself as "conservative and a Christian." He discovered MADA while trying to enhance his social life.

"I had a lot of bad online dates where you sit there with nothing to talk about," he said, describing himself as the type who enjoys "discussing over dinner [more] than going out to the clubs." He found a MADA listing on Meetup and attended his first dinner in the basement of a church in Seattle. He remembers a crowd of twenty to thirty people. They started with small exercises that turned into a larger group discussion. He attended another in-person MADA dinner at a private home, a smaller event that he says was more of a "structured discussion" and "controlled environment." At these first few dinners, he got a sense of "the different flavors" that different hosts brought to MADA, but also saw that the group was united around a "similar theme of sitting down, listening." Drawn in by the in-depth discussions he was having, he decided to host his own dinner for ten to eleven people.

For Mark, who says he loves conversation but is also an introvert, the MADA dinners provided not just a social outlet but also an avenue for expression and community. Many of his friends didn't share his conservative leanings. "For the past several years in the Pacific Northwest, there's an unspoken opinion that you keep your opinions to yourself if you fall into that category." The group gave him a chance not only to express his own views but to challenge them. He says he left his first dinner feeling "excited, not alone."

He went to a few more in-person dinners before he found the MADA Facebook page and started contributing there. He eventually started an in-person MADA chapter in his hometown of Bellevue, Washington, and became a moderator of the online group. "I think I stood out in having a point of view and being curious at the same time," he said. The fact that he had friends with different political views, Justine says, made him a great moderator candidate.

"I would say that [our hosts] who are more conservative either live in more liberal cities or towns or they have family/close friends who are left-leaning. They're more empathetic and understanding because they're exposed, so they can almost act as translators," she said. The idea of translation is an intriguing one: in fact, moderators and admins in the MADA Facebook group often spend time negotiating among different perspectives. Mark says one of his roles is to mediate with the group's conservative members, helping them express themselves more clearly. Sometimes that includes dropping a helpful hint via private Facebook message or stepping into a discussion to draw them out. According to Lisa, who ultimately worked with nearly one hundred individuals, groups, and activists during her time at Facebook, one of the first things MADA did well was "create this role of being a 'bridger,' this identity of people who care about this higher, separate purpose."

Not All Discussions Are Made Equal

Mark said the most challenging subjects for the group have been race, immigration, and abortion. In this, they are not unique. The Facebook group had been live for a little under a year when a member first suggested a poll asking other members when they believed abortion was acceptable. (According to the rules, members can suggest questions, but questions have to be approved by admins to show up on the main MADA discussion page.)

"We thought, 'Hey, this is a good topic,' and we just threw it up there," said Mark. Responses came quickly. Whenever members of the group reply to each other, the moderators get a notification. Watching their notifications come in, Mark said, the moderators realized the discussion might be spinning out of control.

They jumped into the comment thread and posted the following:

> Hi everyone! We recognize that this is a potentially very personal and controversial subject for some in the group. Because of that, our group of moderators will spend extra care checking in and moderating the thread. Thanks, [redacted], for the poll. It's our understanding the idea for this prompt came out of a discussion in another thread last week between [names redacted] on the subject of abortion. Thank you, all, for participating and keeping in mind our ground rules.

Despite jumping in early, Mark says the thread quickly became a "fire out of control." The moderators eventually closed comments.

Justine also remembers this discussion. It was incredibly difficult for her, and changed her perspective and practice as a moderator. Early on in the conversation, under her own name, she posted:

> Are there any women in the group who feel comfortable sharing their thoughts? I want to acknowledge that having this posted by a man and then the first responses being from a few men might make some people feel uncomfortable. When I say some people, I'm including myself.

When they were first developing the in-person dinners, Justine and Tria made a point of clearly defining the facilitator role. They didn't sit at the table with their guests. They didn't share their personal views. These practices created a separation between hosts and participants, an acknowledgment that the two groups answered to different goals. Justine defines the duty of a moderator as follows: "Our main goal is for everyone to feel like they're in a fair, safe environment where they won't be judged." She takes this distinction so seriously, she says, that she even tries to moderate the inadvertent expressions that cross her face during a dinner. "We all respond to things we hear. If I feel something rising in my face—I just pull back."

When opening the Facebook group, she and Tria decided to relax their policy a bit. It was a deliberate departure, influenced by the online format. "We want people to get to know us and the other moderators as contributors, and not just see us as completely neutral robots or rule-enforcers," she said. By expressing their views, they lent their presence in the group a certain familiarity that might otherwise have been lacking. But it also made it harder to figure out where the line between personal and moderator duty lay.

In the abortion thread, not long after the first post under her own name, she posted again, also under her own name:

Men are certainly important in the equation. At the end of the day, though, I'm not sure it can be disputed that it is women and their bodies who experience the pregnancy. And it still bothers me sometimes to see such strong opinions from men about my and other women's bodies, even if they perfectly deserve to have those opinions. It might take time to unpack why that might be. My comment was primarily meant to encourage more women to join the conversation.

In thinking back on it, she acknowledged that part of the moderator's job was moderating her own emotions and expressions online, the same way she moderates her face during an in-person dinner. She's learned that the boundary isn't just about particular topics—although certain topics are particularly hard for her—but rather, a matter of her own emotional state:

There are times when I just start typing, and I realize, "Oh, I'm typing very quickly, and I'm typing with a lot of emotion." Before I hit send I just pause and read it back, edit it, and in that editing, I'm thinking about people [in the group]: how would they interpret what I'm [writing]? What would they interpret as an attack or as an assumption? And so I'll go back and make edits. And the edits are usually, instead of stating opinions as facts, I'll add "I believe," "I think," "I've observed," "In my experience," so it's a little less stating something as though it's a given. When I'm typing, there's that moment to pause before hitting send.

Part of the MADA moderators' philosophy is to reach out to members one-on-one to talk about potential rules infractions, ask about their well-being, and encourage them to moderate the tone of their posts. It's a slow, challenging process of relationship-building, and Justine often has multiple private messages going at once with members of the group. A member messaged her to say he felt like her comments on the abortion thread seemed like bias and possibly favoritism. She considered the feedback and offered to "do better," including stepping back from moderating situations where she might have preexisting relationships or a strong personal bias. It was hard for her, though, she says, since she has strong personal views on the subject. The strength of members' responses indicates the intensity of people's feelings on the topic, but her private messages demonstrate the extent to which those in moderator roles are often held to different standards from participants, both by themselves and by those in their communities.

In a similar future situation, instead of posting a general statement asking "women" to participate, Justine says she would "tag people who I know might have an opinion and sometimes [those people] are women." She said she'd also consider stepping back from moderating discussions that she feels deeply attached to personally. Mark says that the moderators now know that discussions on topics like abortion and race need to be tightly focused, and they'll try to shoot each other a heads-up when approving a question on one of these topics.

Talk Less, Listen More?

Partly in response to discussions like the one above, the moderators proposed an initially controversial new rule, where they asked everyone to limit themselves to one comment per thread per hour. Justine explained that the one-hour rule matches MADA's in-person dialogic principles. "In person, if there are two people who are dominating the conversation, we would interject. We would let it go for a little bit, there is some magic in people being able to feel what they're feeling and be able to express it, but when it gets to the point that people aren't listening, then we interrupt." The same thing was happening in the rapid-fire, often two-person comment exchanges, she continued, as in those rapid in-person conversations. "It's happening so fast it's unclear if they're even reading what the other person wrote."

The group had another discussion about abortion not along ago, Mark says, and he feels it went a lot better. A member suggested the following question:

> I have a sensitive question on several fronts, but my motivation is not to argue about abortion or religion, but to

understand the logic that goes into this position: Many people who hold anti-abortion positions base their positions on Christian scripture (e.g., Jeremiah 1:5; "Before I formed you in the womb I knew you . . .") and yet a sizable proportion of anti-abortion position-holders (I don't have stats) also support certain exceptions, such as when a pregnancy endangers the life of the mother or in cases of rape or incest. I guess I'm wondering how, if you believe some version of the argument of unborn children having inalienable rights or that pregnancy is like the fingerprint of God; a work which is "fearfully and wonderfully made" (Psalm 139:14), how is it also logically consistent to allow for ANY exception, ever? How is the child of rape or incest any less entitled to life than children conceived under other circumstances? Or okay for humans to save an adult woman over a fetus? Or, say, a pregnant 11-year-old girl?—was it not God's jurisdiction to knit life into these wombs?

The question, Mark says, made sense to post because it tackled the topic but in a detailed and specific way. It came at the topic of abortion from the side, asking for theological justification and ideas, rather than asking people outright whether they believed abortion should be legal.

The member who posted the comment, Jess Thida, said the discussion was civil, but she also found it ultimately unsatisfying. "They [the commenters] did not address specifically what seems to be a logical inconsistency, so there was not a good resolution to that question." She joined the group more than a year ago. At the time, she was an American living in Cambodia. She didn't have a lot of American friends around her, and she wanted to talk about politics in a way that went beyond what she saw as the "sensationalism of the media" and the "polarization of my friend group." Most of her questions—like the one above—are her attempts, she says, to understand points of view she doesn't agree with. She credited the moderators with making these conversations possible. "It really comes through that [the moderators] just want to create an open dialogue and a comfortable space for everybody to talk." She enjoys that the group allows people to "connect on a human level without resorting to insults and caricatures."

To Mark, the abortion discussion qualifies as a victory. "I don't care who's right or wrong, but I love that this thread continues for sixty-some people," he said. He also doesn't think the purpose of the group is to change people's point of view. Jess, still a regular participant in MADA conversations, isn't so sure. She wonders: "Why are we spending all this energy arguing our positions if it's not changing anyone's mind?"

Getting Comfortable over Time

After two years together, the tone of the group has started to feel comfortable.

"This is a group of people who have learned how to communicate online. They have a history," Mark said.

Tria, who describes herself as a sensitive person, says she's not sure she'd sign up to moderate an online group if it wasn't

MADA. And yet she also noted to me that the community has grown and changed over time. "Our community understands the tone better, and there are more people following and setting that tone." In a 2019 paper, researchers documented that moderation decisions, over time, "shape community identity."[14] This identity becomes familiar for moderators as well. As the MADA group has established rapport, Tria says, moderation work has become emotionally easier for her.

The group now has close to seven hundred members, and Justine says they've thought about capping it. The discussions function well, and according to Facebook's metrics at the time of this writing, 73 percent of members counted as "active" (a somewhat generous measure that means they'd recently commented, reacted, liked, or even viewed the group's content). Justine spends a lot of time thinking about how to encourage even wider participation. One of their strategies, she says, has been to vary the tone of the content they post throughout the week. At the beginning of the week, the moderators post more pleasant, "getting to know you" questions, things like "What's one item on your to-do list that you've been putting off?" These questions aren't political or issue-based, but the answers are often telling. These questions are great for what Justine describes as "the more shy people."

"That's an entry point for them and they feel comfortable . . . it's harder when it's an issue and you have to be more vulnerable and share your opinion," she said. The moderators have experimented with exercises—similar to the paired discussion from in-person dinners—where they asked participants to private message each other in pairs to get to know each other better. In partnership with Lisa Conn (who no longer works at Facebook, but still builds platforms that facilitate online conversations) they've also tried larger video conversations, in hopes of experimenting with a more real-time format.

The Online Public Citizen

Unlike the country, neither MADA nor Facebook are democracies, and yet, the work that the MADA moderators do is inextricable from their idea of democracy. Tria described her personal connection to the work:

> I think, as the daughter of immigrants, for a long time I felt that outsider feeling . . . there would be people telling me that I didn't belong in the definition of patriotic. And I feel that giving so much time and energy to this organization has made me feel like I am contributing to this country.

Mark, meanwhile, turns to history. Since he began moderating MADA, he says he's started reading up on historical debates and rhetorical strategy, so he can better point out fallacies when they occur in MADA discussions. He admires the relationship between Thomas Jefferson and John Adams, especially the letters they wrote to each other late in their lives, when "they still had reverence for the other person even though they're political foes."

The MADA moderators talk frequently about their biases,

and about how to acknowledge and address them. The moderators have engaged the group on challenging topics, and have polled members on what subjects to include in or exclude from discussion. At the same time, this particular group doesn't practice elections: moderators choose other moderators, and there are layers of responsibility even among moderators. Justine and Tria are the only ones who can decide whether someone can join the group. The next moderator tier, which Mark is a part of, includes people who can approve posts that go into the main discussion, while moderators in the third tier tend to the comments but don't approve members or posts. In this way, the moderator group is its own structured community, with its own rules and practices. They have their own side conversations on Facebook; that's where they give one another a heads-up before approving a potentially controversial post.

Jess describes the MADA moderation style as "heavy," and it is. In the time she spent working with Facebook groups, Lisa says she noticed a trend when it came to how much time moderators spent on their groups: "The more active a mod was, the more time they spent in the group, meant that the group was more civil and had better discourse." She was quick to say that time spent, rather than any particular philosophy, correlated with group civility, but also that defining excellence in moderation was a slippery exercise: "There wasn't one objective definition we used for a better moderator."

Jess does perceive the group as being more conservative than liberal. She recently moved back to the United States, and now lives in a suburb of Boston. She describes herself as more centrist than many of her liberal neighbors, and wonders if that isn't true for her Facebook group, too. "If you were to poll most participants in the group I think you'd find all of us on average are more centrist than the population," she said. "Because we are open-minded enough to come to the middle to discuss with the opposing side, but if you're more rigid in your belief system then it's really hard to find goodness in the other side."

It's hard to say whether the group is more centrist than average. Research has shown that both conservatives and liberals tend to perceive partisans—of both parties—as more extreme than they actually are, and themselves as more alone in their centrism than they actually are.[15] But the same research also suggests that moderates might not be as prone to that bias as stauncher partisans.[16] It's not inherently surprising that an online political discussion group will attract people who have a higher-than-average interest in political conversation, or that a group dedicated to common ground will be more appealing to those who hold moderate views. Justine and Tria mentioned feeling alienated from or frightened of Trump voters after the 2016 election, but Mark and Jess both describe being intrigued by "the other side" long before they joined MADA. Mark had made efforts to seek out wide-ranging political discussions, attending what he describes as a "drunken philosophy" evening at a local bar. It's possible that the people who join MADA are more open to political disagreement to begin with, but it's also possible that the group has shaped and reinforced its own identity over the years.

Surprisingly, who people voted for in 2016—or who they're

voting for in 2020—sometimes seems beside the point. In one recent comment thread, members debated the virtues of an opinion piece by *New York Times* columnist David Brooks, in which Brooks envisioned an imaginary exchange between a Trump opponent and a Trump supporter.[17] An actual exchange, between self-described Trump opponents and supporters, occurred in the comments below the article in MADA. The thread is full of interesting real-life details as to why people voted the way they did, as well as criticism of the way mainstream journalists talk about partisanship.

Acknowledging the group's spirit of openness shouldn't obscure how meticulous the MADA moderators are, and how time-consuming their task continues to be. There are very few comment threads—none that I could find—in which a moderator or admin doesn't make at least one appearance, tending the conversation, watering the seeds of discourse.

In an August 2019 article in the *New Yorker*, journalist Anna Wiener profiles the two moderators of Hacker News, a tech and start-up-focused online forum. She describes the moderators' philosophy as "slow." She doesn't mean it in a negative way. In fact, she compares the Hacker News moderators favorably to moderators on other community platforms and sites:

> On Facebook and YouTube, moderation is often done reactively and anonymously, by teams of overworked contractors; on Reddit, teams of employees purge whole user communities, like surgeons removing tumors. Gackle and Bell, by contrast, practice a personal, focused, and slow

approach to moderation, which they see as a conversational act. They treat their community like an encounter group or Esalen workshop; often, they correspond with individual Hacker News readers over e-mail, coaching and encouraging them in long, heartfelt exchanges.[18]

The MADA moderation philosophy, as expressed to me, seems similar: optimistic in origin and time-consuming in practice. It is "slow" moderation, in that it focuses on individuals and moments. It is conversational, based in shared moments, and it eschews one-size-fits-all categories and descriptions. In order to practice it, in order to believe that the long hours and hard conversations are worth it, the moderators have to believe that they're making important inroads, or suggesting a blueprint for how we can better approach each other as citizens.

MADA is not alone in their goals or their methods, and looking at other groups in this space suggests some commonalities. Better Angels, an in-person movement dedicated to building bridges across the partisan divide, organizes red-blue workshops where the focus is, according to one of their 2018 papers, "Listening and learning rather than declaring and convincing, with a special emphasis on recognizing and admitting concerns about one's own side. The goal is not for people to change their minds about issues, but rather to change their minds about each other." In 2018, Better Angels conducted a survey to understand how participating in these workshops had changed people's views, and found the following: "About 79 percent of participants report that as a result of the experience they are better able to 'understand the experiences, feelings, and beliefs of those on the other side of the political spectrum' and more than 70 percent say that they feel more 'understood by those on the other side of the political divide.'"[19]

Just looking at Justine, Tria, and Mark provides an interesting case study in difference. Mark is gregarious, while Tria is sensitive and Justine is soft-spoken. Their ages and political preferences are fairly wide apart. And yet, what they have in common is a certain personal generosity, evident in their answers to me and to their community. They believe their work is making the world a better place.

From the perspective of creating better citizens, MADA leaves questions unanswered: What happens when groups grow even larger? What about groups where a single arbiter doesn't enforce entry? And what about actual hate, the belief that some people are better or more worthy of participating in our democracy than others? To these large civic questions, MADA doesn't necessarily provide a pat answer, nor does it try to. But it does demonstrate how a small cadre of moderators and members created an online space where several people found a little bit more understanding. If that's your goal, whether on your own private Facebook feed or in a broader discussion, then their model offers some valuable lessons.

2.

Hard Conversations

Pantsuit Nation and Real Talk

When I was researching online comment sections in 2014 and 2015, comment moderators at news organizations constantly told me there was one topic that was especially hard to moderate: race. Several media companies resolved this challenge by limiting or shutting down comments on race-related stories entirely.[1] Stephen Pritchard, then readers' editor at the *Guardian*, wrote about their decision to shut down comments on three specific race and race-related topics:

> Certain subjects—race, immigration, and Islam in particular—attract an unacceptable level of toxic commentary, believes Mary Hamilton, our executive editor, audience. "The overwhelming majority of these comments tend towards racism, abuse of vulnerable subjects, author abuse and trolling, and the resulting conversations below the line bring very little value but

cause consternation and concern among both our readers and our journalists," she said last week.[2]

Since then, the topic has grown more fraught and more difficult to discuss. According to a Pew Research survey published in
2019, a majority of people say that President Trump has worsened
race relations in America, and also that since his election, people
have become more likely to express racist views.[3] The survey also
found that people of different ethnic groups had widely diver-
gent views on race, suggesting how hard it is to find common
ground—or even common spaces for discussion—on the issue.
Which raises the question: What does it mean to try to create
an online community that advocates in favor of racial justice, or
at least greater understanding? In this chapter, I profile two sets
of moderators who have taken very different approaches to this
task, in two very different communities.

Arrival of the Pantsuits

For years, Libby Chamberlain watched Hillary Clinton's political
career from a distance. When Hillary decided to run for president,
Libby wanted ways to show her support. Libby worked as an ad-
missions and career counselor in small-town Maine, and many of
her neighbors supported Bernie Sanders, an earlier Democratic
candidate. Anytime she expressed support for Hillary online, she
faced what she calls "an immediate tear down." One day just a
few weeks before the election, during a break at work, she started
a secret Facebook group called National Pantsuit Day Novem-

ber 8 and invited about thirty of her Hillary-supporting friends from around the country. The description, Libby says, was something like "Wear a pantsuit on election day. You know why." In the interests of privacy, she made it a "secret" group, which means the group wouldn't show up in public Facebook searches, and new members would have to be invited by someone already in the group. She figured they'd get a few photos from different coasts and feel good about it.

She might have underestimated the number of people—many of them women—who, just like her, had been texting their friends about Hillary Clinton. Within a few hours, the group had a thousand members. By the next day, it had twenty-four thousand members. It grew so fast that Libby says Facebook briefly blocked them from accepting new members.

As the group grew, ad hoc, members shaped the tone. A lot of the early content in the group was first-person stories, Libby says. Posts talked about the value of the election, the symbolism of Hillary's characteristic pantsuit, and hopes for the campaign. Libby, who doesn't have a background in digital or offline organizing, noticed that these first-person stories were getting the most engagement, and that this early engagement had a snowball effect—people came into the group and liked these posts, which in turn prompted them to share their own stories. She began to encourage posts focused on positive personal storytelling.

Members and friends reached out to Libby to volunteer as moderators. She accepted pretty much every offer, she says. As the election got closer, she worked with a friend to monitor the group's growth. Once they realized the group was probably going to hit the unheard-of number of two or even three million members, she started looking for more volunteers to moderate, posting appeals on her private Facebook page and keeping close track of the people who contacted her. The initial qualifications for moderation were willingness, time, and proximity. The number of moderators swelled to 190. Volunteers managed everything from post approval to the Pantsuit Nation Twitter feed.

Pantsuit Nation grew so much and so fast that it started getting attention from the mainstream press. Reporters began to ask Libby what the group planned to do after the election. Her response? "We'll figure it out." The night before the election, the group hit two million members. It added a million more on election day itself. Throughout the day, despite early predictions that she'd win easily, it became clear that Hillary would lose. In her concession speech, Hillary referred to supporters in "secret, private Facebook sites," which many interpreted as a reference to Pantsuit Nation.[4] It was an enormous acknowledgment for a Facebook group that hadn't existed six months before. But now the election was over—in heartbreaking fashion, for Hillary's supporters—and the group needed a future.

In December 2016, Libby announced to the group that she had contracted with a publisher to write a Pantsuit Nation book, which would feature stories and images from the group. She also decided to try to create official Pantsuit Nation nonprofits, dedicated to the same liberal causes as Hillary's candidacy.

Disagreement in the vast but fledgling group was swift and public. While some members were supportive of Libby's decisions, others were upset that private posts would be published. The book deal and subsequent controversy were written up in several news outlets, including the *New York Times*.[5] Libby adjusted to the criticism, clarifying that the only people whose posts and photos would be reprinted in the book would be those who'd given permission. The book came out in May 2017.

More than two years later, I bought it. It's physically beautiful, with a dense blue hardback cover and pages of full-color photographs. The bulk of it—outside of Libby's introduction—is the personal stories of Pantsuit Nation members. These stories are uplifting, positive, well packaged. One member, Laurel Ann from Florida, talks about finding acceptance in the group after spending her whole life voting Republican: "I felt like I belonged. Even when discussing some of my views that are still rather conservative, I was respected." Others talk about their own or their parents' immigrant journeys; the power of voting for the first time; or the joy of finally being able to marry their same-sex partner. In the introduction, Libby foregrounds the book with a message of inclusivity:

> They [the stories in the book] illustrate, achingly, the effects of systemic racism, ableism, homophobia and xenophobia, and they are a clarion call for intersectional feminists of every class, shade, gender, nationality, religion and ethnicity to join together in resistance.[6]

In her time in Pantsuit Nation, she writes, she came to realize the pantsuit "could represent everything from a doctor's scrubs to a military uniform to a hijab." It's an uplifting metonym, but perhaps too easy and too broad for a group of Pantsuit Nation's size. Within the group, divisions began to emerge.

In a 2016 article in the *Nation*, journalist Sarah Seltzer described the beneficial effects of Pantsuit Nation's brand of personal testimony:

> Transgender, Muslim, and Latina members have asked fellow Pantsuiters to stand with them in the face of hate and discrimination, and received tens of thousands of supportive comments in response. . . . Nearly everyone who speaks up is flooded with loving comments.[7]

Libby told me that survivors of sexual assault, who often have a difficult time sharing their stories online, have told her they also found the group therapeutic. It's one of the things she's proudest of, and her moderation guidelines enforce it—questioning survivors' stories is grounds for dismissal.

But other members spoke up to challenge how the group, which in theory focuses on inclusivity, handled conversations around race and justice. Writer, blogger, and group member Jenina Marie, who identifies as a woman of color, wrote a blog post drawing attention to a culture that she felt ignored marginalized members' stories:

> The tone of the page is self-centered as fuck and congratulatory. Congratulatory for what? I'm not sure. There are so few stories from the most marginalized groups, I wondered what the point actually was.[8]

In an article on *HuffPost*, group member Harry Lewis expressed disappointment:

> Moreover, Pantsuit Nation has devolved into a space where white people can claim to fight for the survival of the sisterhood by performing apolitical acts of self-humanizing. Instead of doing tangible work, like running for office or even making phone calls to local representatives, white people treat minorities as props in their self-congratulatory posts about being inclusive, loving people and watch as everyone congratulates them for being decent, passive human beings. It does this on the backs of people of color whose lives are directly and disproportionately affected by Trump's policies yet are read as "fake" or "insincere" in their performance of grief and fear.[9]

The Reverend Rebecca Black, an Episcopal priest and member of the group (she's white) gave an example of a conversation that she found troubling. A member made a post and labeled it for "women of color." The response, Rebecca says, was "melting down," much of it by white members who felt that they were being unfairly barred from participating. Although I didn't find the initial post Rebecca was referring to, I did find another one in which moderators talked about closing comments on a thread about race. In their statement, they noted: "Even in groups, like ours, that are liberal and whose members consider themselves aware and attuned to systemic racism and white supremacy, there will be perpetuation of those very same oppressions by and toward other members." The post got nearly forty thousand responses. Some expressed support for the moderators' message. But in others, commenters expressed frustration at what they perceived as divisive rhetoric on the part of the group's critics.

Focusing on Moderation

In the spring of 2017, Pantsuit Nation's leaders hired one of their volunteer moderators—Grace Caldara—as director of engagement. Grace has a PhD in chemical biology and a passion for teaching. She also has a history of helping online groups have tough conversations about race.

The move was part of a shift in the organization's moderation strategy. At the time of the election, Pantsuit Nation had an enormous corps of volunteer moderators, but these volunteers occasionally made what Libby describes as "mistakes." For example, one volunteer Twitter moderator started blocking all dissenters. This might work for a small group of friends, but it's a policy that didn't work for a group that, in Libby's words, had suddenly become "a very publicly recognized name." Libby described her thought process after the election:

It was like wait a second, who are all these people? They're all over the world, didn't have a training process. There were some mistakes that we made as a community early on because there was no cultural competency understanding broadly across our moderation teams.

There were people doing things as moderators on behalf of the organization . . . They just didn't know any better.

She began to pare down the number of moderators, and to think about how to build cultural competency. Within a few weeks, the moderation team was down to about one hundred people, and eventually, to twelve, a number that she says is "more manageable." With the exception of Grace, the moderators are still volunteers. Their core policies haven't changed. The mods reinforce the focus on personal storytelling, but they are more selective. They now approve about ten posts per day out of the hundreds that they receive. These posts, Libby says, need to be original content, in which the poster talks about something they have personally experienced. They've tried to steer away from what she calls "ally cookie" stories, where white people post about how they've stood up for more marginalized folks. This is something she's learned over time from group members.

Grace started moderating Facebook groups after her first child was born, when she joined a group about babywearing. Babywearing is a practice in which parents carry their babies close to their bodies in slings or other carrying devices like Baby-Björns. Babywearing has existed for centuries in many cultures. Online, Grace noticed that several discussions in the babywearing group devolved into angry threads over what did or didn't qualify as cultural appropriation. Impressed with the way Grace fielded difficult questions about vaccines, the moderators of the group invited her to become an admin. Grace identifies as a woman of color, and one of her early goals was to help create a space where other babywearers of color felt comfortable. To that end, she crafted a series of guidelines. As she described the process:

> I wrote a social justice statement that said very firmly what our values were within the group when it came to trying to support other babywearers of color which was "we believe that racism is a problem and it's systematic and systemic," "we believe racism is prejudice plus power," and we spelled out exactly what cultural appropriation was and why it was wrong.

Grace says some people called her racist, and a few members left the group. But she also received messages of support from other community members, who told her that her posts had taught them something. She remembers a long response she typed to a thread about infant ear piercing. In her post, she talked about how she viewed piercing ears as a way to reconnect with her grandparents' lost culture. Later, a member reached out privately to tell her that her comment had helped them see the issue differently.

Like a lot of first-time moderators, she says one of her early surprises was how time-consuming it was. She'd spend hours glued to her phone, afraid to let the community down. She felt personally responsible, but she also gained a reputation as a moderator who embraced difficult conversations.

Shortly after the election, she wrote a post in Pantsuit Nation. She explained how they'd laid out social justice guidelines in the babywearing group, and provided helpful links. She says she knew it wasn't a "typical post," but thought it might be helpful with some of the issues the group was having. Because posts needed to be approved by admins in order to be published, she reached out to a friend from high school who was on the Pantsuit Nation moderation team. "I said 'Hey, I put this post in, approve it, don't approve it, whatever,'" she said. She got a response: the moderators liked her post, and they wanted her to join the moderation team as a volunteer.

She says one of her early goals was to understand some of the frustration in the group.

"We had a lot of frustrated women of color at that time, and rightfully so, and it was a lot of trying to figure out how can we make this a better, more inclusive place. It was a lot of late nights," she said. Grace and the other moderators talked extensively over Facebook Messenger, trying to figure out "how can we provide our members with opportunities for education."

By this point, Grace had realized that she didn't want to go back to doing research in the isolated confines of a lab. She was planning to become a science teacher when Libby asked if she'd consider a role with Pantsuit Nation instead. "I found that this was a very unique way to reach lots of people and to try to make the world a little bit better," she said. She accepted, and became the nonprofit's first director of engagement, responsible for the entire moderation team and the ongoing moderation strategy.

She worked with the team to develop ways to "de-escalate" tense conversations. Usually, she says, moderators don't get tagged into threads until "shit hits the fan." By that point, a moderator's role in a thread is to prevent further damage. Grace started pulling together tools and sample phrases for moderators to use, things like "I understand where you're coming from, but here are some of the things that are really wrong with what you just said," or "I'm sorry this terrible thing happened to you, but it's not an example of xyz." She focused on providing resources around social justice, racism, and intersectionality. From there, she said, these tools evolved into something more structured, a formal moderator training program:

It morphed into more of a training where we talked about some of the common things we have to step into, how do we defuse it. And then also what's really important—and what a lot of people forget—is that it's okay to step away. As mods, you don't always take care of yourself, and asking for help, for somebody else to come in, is really important. When I was in the babywearing group . . . it would have really helped to know that it would be okay if I stepped away. When you're dealing with sensitive and difficult topics, sometimes they're really personal to you or you've had personal experiences, and it can really hit home. Those are really hard to deal with. It all boils down to one of our earlier mottoes; somebody had said it at some point: "Be the change you want to see in the comments." Be the one that's coming in and trying to provide education and coming from a place of understanding yet still also supporting the person who's being hurt by whatever comment you're moderating.

Grace's philosophy toward moderator training includes a few key principles:

- Providing tools and sample phrases for de-escalating tense situations
- Emphasizing education, particularly providing resources to community members around issues related to social justice and marginalization
- Moderator self-care and emotional "coping"—ways to address the personal impact of difficult conversations, and to tap into team members and a personal support network to help

Grace says they've run the training program a couple of times. Before it starts, moderators get a training document that outlines protocol and expectations. The next phase, which usually happens over the phone, introduces moderators to Pantsuit Nation's history and to frequently asked questions. In the third and final phase, they work together online: she shows in-the-moment examples from the group's comments, and they talk through how best to moderate them. Moderators also get a worksheet containing real-life examples of past conversations. They suggest how they'd moderate the thread, and then talk over their responses with Grace.

Other forms of moderator training, although not always formalized in a program, mention similar techniques. Moderators might frame de-escalation in different ways—they might talk about compassion, goal-setting, or putting out fires. But the experience is consistent: a moderator gets pulled into a fight, and has to calm everybody down and restore order and, in some cases, a sense of common purpose.

And then there's self-care, or the practice of moderators protecting themselves from the emotional harm of caring for others' feelings constantly. In some groups, like the MADA group featured in an earlier chapter, I heard moderators talk about self-care as stepping back from situations where they exhibited personal bias, or being cognizant of their own hot-button issues. Justine and Tria, the founders of MADA, often moderated dinners where guests expressed views the two of them found personally difficult to hear. This was especially true, Justine said, when guests talked about gender and immigration. Justine would keep her face impassive while moderating, but afterward, she and Tria would send each other images of the inadvertent funny faces they made. This kind of private messaging let them bond over the difficulties of the job, and also served as a way of sharing values and releasing tension. In other groups, moderators might take breaks or tag in colleagues.[10] Sometimes more experienced moderators helped newer ones with self-care by reminding them to step aside to avoid getting burned out.[11]

Self-care comes up most often for moderators who deal with issues of identity. These conversations are difficult to begin with. Online abuse is also not distributed evenly. A study by Amnesty International, which analyzed millions of tweets received by women in the US and UK throughout 2017, concluded that "Black women received 60% more problematic tweets and 84% more abusive tweets compared to white women. Most of the abuse was racist (70% more than white women)."[12]

For a moderator, especially one who identifies as a person of color, introducing sensitive topics into an online environment can be a delicate act. A few of Grace's past posts illustrate the care, as well as the visibility, that come with her role in the community: her posts are several paragraphs long, studded with links and illustrated with photos. In one, she responds to the suggestion that women should kneel during the national anthem to show solidarity with Christine Blasey Ford, who testified that then US Supreme Court nominee Brett Kavanaugh had assaulted her. Grace wrote:

> Co-opting the movement of kneeling distracts from the original intent and message and morphs it into something else: white women co-opting a black movement against police brutality and turning it into a protest centering on themselves.

In other posts, Grace links to stories that other marginalized members have posted, boosting their messages and requests for support.

Lecia Michelle, a librarian, journalist, and woman of color, joined the pantsuited ranks pretty soon after the group started. She's also a writer and blogger who's written several *Medium* articles about race and how to have tough conversations about race. She praises Grace's approach, even while noting that she's been dissatisfied with the way discussions about race have gone in Pantsuit Nation. "I think that she's the only person that really tries," she said.

Getting Real

In December 2016, Lecia and two friends started their own Facebook group to provide a space for discussing race. The group was intended partly as a response to their own frustrating experiences as women of color in Pantsuit Nation. They called it Real Talk: WOC & Allies for Racial Justice and Anti-Oppression. It now has 1,191 members. They attracted initial members by recruiting in Pantsuit Nation. Rebecca Black, whom I mentioned above, joined Real Talk early on after learning about it in Pantsuit Nation.

From the beginning, Lecia's goal was to create a space that focused on discussions of race, but from the perspective of women of color. Real Talk is run by women of color—they form the majority of the member base, and Lecia intends to keep it that way. A core precept, in order to participate, is committing to active anti-racism. Lecia has an unflinching openness when it comes to confronting racism. "You have a lot of well-meaning white liberals who flat-out will not talk about race, and if you bring it up, they'll be like 'We're all in this together, and race shouldn't matter right now.'"

She says she's been in conversations where people will say things like "I don't see color," or "Why are you focusing on color?" For Lecia, racism transcends politics—it's a structural issue that affects everyone, and comments like "I don't see color" erase the unique experiences of people of color. In one of her *Medium* posts, she criticized white women who don't challenge racism among their friends and neighbors. In another post, she offered strong words for nonblack people of color:

The notion that black people don't experience pain at the level of white people still exists in today's medicine. So I can't help but think this idea has bled over into society, where both white and nonblack people of color (NBPOC) have bought into it.[13]

In other words, in Real Talk, good intentions aren't enough. Moderators expect action and dialogue. They're not interested in scale—in fact, they actively reject it. Every so often, Lecia goes through the member list and culls "lurkers"—people who belong to the group but never post or comment.

The group's organizing metaphor is one of a "home." In posts, people—especially longtime members—refer to the group as a "house." A welcome post is titled "house rules" instead of "community guidelines." Once members are granted entry, they enter the living room, which is the main hall of the house. A sidebar explains the group's purpose:

"Real Talk: WOC and Allies" is a space where allies can come to ask questions, find resources and have discussions about what they can do to truly be an ally. We welcome cis women, transgender women or anyone self-identifying as a woman. The group strives to be diverse in every way and to embrace and support the fact that we are all connected through the intersectionality of our unique backgrounds.

From the living room, members can use links in the sidebar

to enter several specific subgroups, or rooms, all part of the Real Talk family. The subgroups have names like "The Library" (for resources and links), "The Parlour," and the "The Gym" (for training, which will come up again shortly). Facebook's platform doesn't make it easy to create this type of discussion-within-a-discussion. "The Mending Room," for example, is organized as a series of "events" that members go to, and every so often, the moderators open a new one. It's hard to chase down these groups; it occurred to me while doing so that it wouldn't be a bad idea for Facebook to make the process easier.

The living room is the main gathering space, the heart of the house, where all members mix. In one recent post, members discussed whether dressing kids up as Moana—or really, in any Halloween costume based on a specific culture—is offensive. In another, a member shared a heartbreaking story of her confusion when a neighbor decided to include a lynched skeleton as a part of his Halloween décor. In the comments, members shared suggestions for how to deal with the situation. In a third post, women debated whether or not black and white women can be real friends.

Lecia and Rebecca both told me that participating in Real Talk is meant to be a challenging experience. When members petition to join Real Talk, they have to say whether they identify as a white woman or a woman of color. A key part of gaining entry into the house, for white women, is completing a two-week "allyship" training program that Lecia and Rebecca have developed. Here's how Lecia described the course's goals, again from one of her *Medium* posts:

Real Talk offers one of the few programs of its kind. You have the opportunity to ask all those dumb questions you want to ask but have been too afraid to do so. You will get answers, and you will also get a thorough explanation as to why your question is problematic. If you want the tools to have a discussion with your racist relatives over Christmas dinner, the mentors will provide those tools to you. Each mentor has been where you are. They're the first to tell you that they still screw up. This isn't about seeking perfection. This is about seeking knowledge. . . . This isn't about good or bad white women. Let me put that another way: THERE ARE NO GOOD AND BAD WHITE WOMEN.[14]

Lecia's argument, of course, is that everyone exists somewhere along the racism spectrum. This is true not just for white women, but also for women of color, who are also expected to join in conversations about internalized racism.

"We've had interesting—not fun—conversations about colorism," said Lecia. (Colorism is a term for when people of the same race or ethnicity discriminate against one another based on differences in skin tone. It happens in many societies around the world.) "We've had conversations about privilege, and those are hard, and then also internalized racism; we've had that talk several times."

Rebecca, who designed the training, is an ordained Episcopal priest, and anti-racism is one of the three pillars of her ministry. When Real Talk began, several of the group moderators noticed that there were common things white women were saying in the group—like asserting they couldn't be racist because they had friends who were people of color, or dominating conversations with their viewpoint—that violated the group's mission as a place that focuses on women of color's experiences. Rebecca suggested developing special online anti-racism training for prospective group members. She figured she could draw on similar training she had helped conduct in her day job.

The Real Talk trainings take place in one of the special "rooms" of the house, known—fittingly—as The Gym. Participants go through the training in cohorts, and the curriculum includes homework assignments, active discussion, and role-playing difficult conversations. The training begins by defining racism at four levels: structural, institutional, interpersonal, and personal, said Rebecca. The group talks about white privilege and white fragility. Rebecca said that trainees may feel attacked or even threatened during the process. This is where mentors—other white women who have gone through the training—take on a role. Trainees are paired with mentors, who share their experiences. The organizers tell trainees to "sit with" their feelings of defensiveness; "Live with it, learn from it," Rebecca said. She described the trainers' methods and past experience:

> Every single one of us has had an experience of thinking "No, I'm one of the ones who knows stuff" or "I have tons of friends of color and I know what I'm doing," and none of us do. We have been brought up in a culture that has privileged us and taught us a certain way of being and to learn a new way of being is so incredibly hard, it takes constant work.

In addition to group conversations, participants also complete homework assignments. In one assignment, participants are asked to take an "implicit bias" test. The test, developed by researchers, measures respondents' innate preferences: for example, whether they have a preference for a particular skin tone. They're encouraged not to be afraid of their results, no matter what those results are; everything is a learning opportunity. Then, participants read an academic article about racial microaggressions and watch an explainer video on YouTube. In another homework assignment, participants read about white fragility, then reflect what situations and conversations trigger their own feelings of white fragility. The training takes two weeks, and they run it roughly once a month.

Lecia requires the training for white women who want to join Real Talk, but they also offer it to anyone who's interested for a $35 fee. The money goes toward a fund that they disburse to members in need. They've extended the training beyond Real Talk: Rebecca told me they've trained the executive boards of other nonprofits that do online community building. In all, Rebecca estimates that they've trained four hundred to five hundred women. "I would love to start sending men through this training," she said with a laugh. Lecia said she's also offered it to the admin team at Pantsuit Nation, although they preferred to come up with their own. Not everyone finishes the program.

"We really try to work deep; we're not offering a surface-level experience," Rebecca said. "That's not something that everybody is ready for." When they started offering it to other nonprofit organizations, they noticed a high initial dropout rate, which prompted Lecia to write a blog post encouraging people to stick with it. "My message to white women: Don't let another white person tell you something you know a WOC won't. If we're unconvinced of your good intentions toward us, that's all that should matter to you," she wrote.

Over time, Rebecca says she's grown to appreciate the value of conducting this training online, instead of in-person. Online conversations—at least, text-based ones—lack conversational cues, like vocal tone or gesture, that set important context. But in-person conversations also come with the expectation of immediate response. Rebecca says giving people a little bit more space to process is actually helpful in training. "It gives people a chance to think and sit back a little, to listen first and not have to react in the moment." She herself is part of what she describes as a "white women's affinity group," where she said they work through, among other things, how they benefit from structural racism and privilege. The six members have been meeting for four years, and although she's met only two of them in person, she says they're "emotionally" very close and have "shared many of our life events with one another." "There's a belief that you can't have relationships with people unless you see them in person. I don't think that's true," she told me.

One of the other important things that women do in the training is role-play a type of restorative interaction that Lecia refers to as "mending." Real Talk has a dedicated Mending Room. A lot of things can get someone called into The Mending Room. For a white woman, making a casual statement like "I understand racism because my husband's black" can get her called in. In the room, she'll interact one-on-one with a mentor who'll explain why her statement might be harmful. Sometimes she'll agree and return to the main group, an apology at the ready. Sometimes, Lecia says, she'll leave Real Talk instead. Individual conversations in The Mending Room can run upward of fifty comments.

Lecia says that being called into The Mending Room is not a punishment. People may go through the mending process many, many times over the course of their time in the group. "The word we use is they do it with 'grace,'" she said. "You're doing it in a way that respects the conversation that's in mending and also respects the process, because the process has to be . . . educational." During the training period, white women get the chance to practice mending, playing the role of both the transgressor and the mentor, so they're prepared for when it actually happens.

Both in The Mending Room and the training program, white women will mentor other white women. The goal is twofold, says Lecia: white women listen to each other more readily than they do to women of color, and it saves a woman of color from doing the emotional work of explaining, often repeatedly, why a particular comment was harmful to her.

When it comes to online conversations about race, the entire internet could use a mending room. When vitriol and hate speech pop up, organizations don't know how to handle it, and staffers tasked with moderating comment sections get frustrated, burned out, or both. Over time, in response to demand from members, Real Talk has also started a training program for nonblack women of color. Less structured, this training runs on-demand, and focuses on generational trauma and providing mental health resources for people of color, in addition to emphasizing harms that members of the group may commit against others. This training isn't required for entry, but it's available to people who want it or to people who the moderators think might benefit.

Real Talk is a house with many, many rooms; each with its own rules, conventions, and population. Not everyone has access to every room. Being able to divide up the rooms and the audiences is essential to achieving Real Talk's purpose, as the house rules make clear:

> We want to also respect the fact that WOC and their allies do not necessarily share the same language on these sensitive topics. There may be times where we need to educate each other so that we can move on to more meaningful dialogue.

Members can designate certain posts "for women of color only." Sometimes these policies cause controversy, which the house rules go on to provide some remedy for:

> 9.   We understand that each person may have different backgrounds and those backgrounds can make someone more or less sensitive to posts. We want to encourage all participation, as each member needs. If you need to post something and would like to limit it to only WOC or only ALLIES, please use the phrase (WOC ONLY) or (ALLIES ONLY) before your post to indicate that only women of color or only allies are supposed to respond.

10. With that being said, we know that these WOC ONLY conversations may trigger discussion among allies on posts they are not allowed to comment on. If you are a non-WOC/ally and you would like a safe space to discuss any WOC ONLY topic, head over to this thread: [redacted]. This group is meant to be an open discussion space for anyone who would like to be a part of it (WOC and ALLIES).

Members are encouraged to organize on one another's behalf, including financially. When one member posted about getting poor care in a local hospital, Lecia told me another group member drove to the hospital and had a conversation with the staff. The group also hosts funding drives, rooted in the conviction that the community must help each other. They have a woman of color fund that members can contribute to, that goes to help other members. (This is also where the training money goes.) People have asked for help paying their utility bills in a particularly difficult year. One member needed a new motorized wheelchair but couldn't afford it, so the group chipped in.

Some groups balk at the idea of hosting fund-raisers, but giving is an important part of Lecia's definition of justice. "I'm sure we've been lied to," Lecia said. "But either you're giving or you're not." The group exists on trust, on an all-encompassing vision of the social contract. Either you're helping or you're not. Either you're working to become an ally or you're not. This approach is not for everyone. "It is OK if you feel like this isn't the right fit for you," the house rules say.

While Lecia expressed frustration with the way some conversations about race have gone in Pantsuit Nation, she also notes that one of Grace's challenges is moderating a group of 3.2 million people. In that sense, the existence of a spin-off group is not inherently a bad thing—in fact, it might be a valuable adaptation as groups scale and individual members reclaim or re-envision the group's purpose. In an article in the *New York Times*, the researcher Zizi Papacharissi, who has studied and written about social networks, expressed that sentiment to journalist Jonah Engel Bromwich, telling him: "The best way to react to that [group] growth is not to pack up and leave but create these microgroups within the larger organization that continue to communicate."[15] Pantsuit Nation has spawned several spin-offs. Some of these are local chapters of Pantsuit Nation, which would fit neatly into Zizi's model. Others, like Real Talk and the nonaffiliated Pantsuit Revolution, tweak the message. They're not exactly micro-groups, or at least they don't exist under the Pantsuit Nation umbrella, but members of Real Talk do continue to communicate back to Pantsuit Nation.

The relationship between Pantsuit Nation and Real Talk might also serve a valuable democratic purpose, namely, providing for different "public spheres" that challenge and overlap with each other on an issue of public interest. The public sphere, first suggested by the philosopher Jürgen Habermas, has become a profoundly influential concept: it's a discussion space where citizens can gather and talk about common concerns. In Habermas's original philosophy, this was a space marked by equality, where citizens would check their societal privileges and differences at the door. In practical reality, of course, it isn't possible to so conveniently dispense with convention. In her profoundly influential essay "Rethinking the Public Sphere," the feminist theorist Nancy Fraser suggested we need many different publics, some of them specifically for minority groups to negotiate identity:

> Members of subordinated social groups—women, workers, peoples of color, and gays and lesbians—have repeatedly found it advantageous to constitute alternative publics. I propose to call these *subaltern counterpublics* in order to signal that they are parallel discursive arenas where members of subordinated social groups invent and circulate counterdiscourses, which in turn permit them to formulate oppositional interpretations of their identities, interests, and needs.[16]

In this context, rather than being divisive, Lecia and team are developing a counterdiscourse, an intervention that critiques and opposes a mainstream online discussion about racial identity.

At the very least, both of these examples demonstrate that there is an alternative to turning off the comments, but this alternative is a difficult and challenging road to travel, one that requires preparation and practice. For organizations that can't invest in moderation, it might make sense to avoid opening discussions on topics like race. Organizations that are committed to dialogue will need to think hard about what types of discussions to create, who enters them, and who moderates them. Moderating online conversations is emotionally difficult—and not just because of trolling and harassment. The work required to develop cultural competency, to explain social justice issues, to navigate personal identity in a public space, and to manage moderators' emotions can take a toll. Groups that discuss identity must think meaningfully about how and where they divide those burdens.

The investment required to create these types of conversations may be significant, but so is the reward. Grace's moderation philosophy is built on individual relationships, and a teacher's patient, ripple-effect theory of change:

> My goal in some ways was to change the world. . . . I believe in trying to reach that one person. If I can get them to try to change how they think of something or how they see the world, they can take that and bring it to their friends and family. How do I reach that one person, either plant the seed or water it a little, get it to grow just a little bit more?

3.

All in the Neighborhood

Nextdoors, NUMTOTs, and More

Sometime in the mid-2000s, Peggy Robin, the admin of a local LISTSERV for the Washington, DC, neighborhood of Cleveland Park, started to notice something was off about the posts being submitted by purported city council candidates. Not only were the posts absurdly offensive—racist and pornographic—they were coming in fast and thick. Even trolls, she knew, struggled to be so prolific and so rude at the same time. She eventually began to suspect that one of the candidates for city council was impersonating his opponents, submitting gross comments to the LISTSERV in hopes of damaging their chances in the upcoming election.

It's not exactly how Peggy dreamed of getting involved in local government back when she started the LISTSERV with her then-husband, Bill Adler, in 1999. Then, they'd hoped the LISTSERV could connect people who cared about the community. She'd grown up near Washington, DC, gone to college in California, and moved to Cleveland Park a couple of years afterward, in 1977. She got involved in neighborhood organizing when someone slipped a note under her door about an upcoming community meeting. She and Bill, inspired by a similar LISTSERV in the neighboring community of Adams Morgan, used a free service called ONElist, which would eventually be purchased by Yahoo, to set up the LISTSERV for Cleveland Park.

To get the word out, the two of them printed flyers and passed them around at the local swimming pool. Within a few days, she says, their group had several hundred members. By the end of its second year it had two thousand, and has grown by about a thousand members every year since, largely via word of mouth. At its height, the group claimed more than eighteen thousand members. This is an impressive tally, considering the combined population of Ward 3, the DC district that includes Cleveland Park and several other neighborhoods, is a little over eighty-two thousand.[1] At one point, Peggy said administrators at Yahoo told her that the Cleveland Park LISTSERV was one of the largest neighborhood groups on their platform.

Several years after the group was started, Yahoo executives flew Peggy and several other Yahoo group admins out to company HQ in Sunnyvale, California, to ask them about how to make the Groups product even better.

"We gave them all kinds of suggestions, and they didn't take any of them," Peggy said.

This might explain why, just weeks before its twentieth birthday, the Cleveland Park LISTSERV faces the biggest technological challenge of its existence. After years of dwindling support,

Yahoo finally decided to shut down most of the features and functionality associated with Yahoo Groups, including the ability to upload polls, files, shared calendars, and photos. Existing groups will become email-only, which means that files, photos, and other content will disappear, as will some moderator functionality. People who want to join groups will still be able to search the site and email other members, but that's about it. The announcement was made less than a month before the changes were due to take effect, which left group owners—including Peggy—scrambling to find alternatives.

Over the years, Yahoo Groups has lost out to Facebook, Twitter, and other social media competitors. But as was pointed out on Twitter and in news articles after the shutdown was announced, Yahoo Groups hosted formative moments in the internet's history.[2] And there are still groups like Peggy's that rely on Yahoo Groups. In one article, *Verge* journalist Bijan Stephen noted that some of the UK's crucial national telephone infrastructure is still administered via a Yahoo group.[3] An article on *Vice* quotes a Reddit user wondering how to download their Yahoo group: "a lot of the information and discussion there isn't replaceable."[4] The Yahoo Groups shutdown highlights one of the fundamental vulnerabilities of groups hosted on private platforms: companies can shutter them for business reasons, giving users little to no notice that entire swaths of content will disappear. For neighborhood groups, that content includes archives of years of neighborhood events and meetings, maps of past streets, photos of bygone storefronts, and other valuable information. Yahoo has done this before—in 2009, the company shut down the hosting service GeoCities, taking years' worth of web history with it.[5]

Peggy has spent the past few weeks finding a new home for the group—a service called Groups.io—and painstakingly migrating members and content over. In the process, she's discovered that nearly four thousand email addresses she had on her list had gone inactive in the past twenty years. Reading the email extensions—@compuserve, @prodigy—feels like a walk down internet memory lane. The email list is now around 14,500 members, but Peggy says that she knows these email addresses are active. She has no plans to discontinue the group—if anything, she wants to maintain and possibly even expand it.

Peggy's learned a lot about how you run a neighborhood group, as well as about the neighborhood. She's learned how to organize search parties for lost pets, calm tensions when one neighbor accuses another of not scooping up after their dog, and what kinds of posts should never see the light of day. For example, the issue of people impersonating others? A surprisingly common one for her neighborhood LISTSERV. Sometimes, she'll get posts from a suspiciously satisfied customer, linking to a local business. Then, she'll open her inbox and see the exact same post—but with the name of the customer changed—appearing in the LISTSERV of another DC neighborhood (she subscribes to several DC neighborhood LISTSERVs). She calls this practice "shilling," and it's severe enough that over the years she's developed a zero-tolerance policy for it: advertisers who are caught shilling are forever banned from advertising on the LISTSERV. "What am I, an idiot?" she asked.

Another common problem: people accusing their neighbors of criminal behavior. This has two sides: sometimes people will accuse a known neighbor of criminal activity; other times, they'll share unconfirmed reports of "suspicious" behavior.

"Do they not understand they can get sued for this?" Peggy wonders, of the first. Peggy has a policy that all posts must be approved by a moderator before being sent out to the group, thanks in part to a past controversy in which groups of Florida activists began spamming the Cleveland Park LISTSERV. She says she'll usually only approve crime posts if the crimes are a matter of public police record.

When it comes to reporting so-called suspicious behavior, it's gotten other neighborhood message boards into trouble in the past. "I've certainly been accused of enabling racism because people have complained about black kids in mostly white neighborhoods," she said. (She's quick to add that she's constantly being accused of bias by various LISTSERV subscribers; it's one of the perils of the job.) Cleveland Park is a majority-white neighborhood, in a rapidly changing city. Racial profiling has been a major concern for community LISTSERVs and online groups, both in DC and nationally. In 2015, a private messaging service in the nearby Washington, DC, neighborhood of Georgetown was shut down over concerns that it had essentially become a vehicle for racial profiling and discrimination.[6]

In 2016, social networking company Nextdoor, which runs several hyper-local online groups and message boards, started experimenting with new tools to reduce racial bias in crime reports after multiple complaints that "it has become a magnet for racial profiling, leading African-American and Latino residents to be seen as suspects in their own neighborhoods," according to an article in the *New York Times*.[7] The irony of Nextdoor's racial profiling was not lost on the author of the article: "Website Meant to Connect Neighbors Hears Complaints of Racial Profiling." Among other things, Nextdoor leadership planned to add tools that required users to fill out information beyond race when making a report of suspicious behavior.

In a nod to changing technology, Peggy's relaxed her rule a little bit, and now allows people to post videos taken by their video doorbells of packages being stolen off their stoops.

She says that some of her favorite posts are the ones in which the LISTSERV helps neighbors recover lost pets. She's also proud of some of the in-depth conversations the LISTSERV has enabled among neighbors. Nearly two decades ago, she says the LISTSERV provided a valuable outlet for both pro-development and anti-development factions who were arguing over the appearance of a proposed Giant supermarket. Eventually, the two sides came to an agreement, and the dates of town hall and citizens committee meetings on the subject were widely shared on the LISTSERV. Every year for the past several years, she's written an end-of-year blog post highlighting the best long-running discussions in the group, and 2018's second runner-up was a multipart exchange between several neighbors, ostensibly helping one of them convince an acquaintance why she should vote. Among other things, neighbors cited the influence of elections over local affairs, the value of self-governance, and the fact that DC residents didn't even get the right to vote in presidential elections until the early 1960s. The discussion, called "Why Vote," narrowly lost the "Best Long-Running Discussion Thread" crown to "Red Fox." One neighbor kicked off that discussion by mentioning that they'd spotted a red fox in their neighborhood. Others chimed in with their own red fox sightings, mostly positive. One neighbor offered a pithy praise of foxes, including a stab at DC's other backyard wildlife: "We will not even mention the rudeness and rapaciousness of the deer."

One of the reasons that the Cleveland Park LISTSERV has grown so vast is because of the care that the moderator—Peggy—puts into it.

"They don't just accept whatever's written; sometimes they intervene with some very helpful suggestions," said Therese Fergo, a Realtor who's been living in Cleveland Park for the past twenty years and estimates she's been on the LISTSERV for fifteen of them. She's used the LISTSERV to find contractors and comment on local issues. She's noticed that Peggy likes to have fun: for example, around April Fool's Day, she publishes a fake post that can be quite provocative, something about changing the parking payment system on a busy neighborhood street, for example. Or sometimes, in a roundup of local events, Peggy will toss in a fake event. Therese says this is "fun and engaging," although no word on whether people ever showed up thinking a fake event was real. Therese has gone to happy hours hosted by the LISTSERV, and even met up with LISTSERV moderator Bill when she visited Japan (where he now lives). She's also had people recognize her at local stores based on things she's posted. "It's really created a very strong community and a very reliable community," she said.

Peggy says the LISTSERV is one of the few local outlets that follow hyper-local issues, not just fox sightings but also DC's neighborhood advisory committee meetings. These cover issues too small-scale for a big news organization, even the nearby *Washington Post*. A local newspaper, the *Northwest Current*, used to fill the gap, she says, but the *Current* went bankrupt in early January 2018 and ceased publication altogether in mid-2019. According to an October 2018 news story on the industry site Poynter, "about 20 percent of all metro and community newspapers in the United States—about 1,800—have gone out of business or merged since 2004."[8] Peggy says the LISTSERV has stepped into the space.

Connecting neighborhoods is a big business opportunity. Nextdoor, the network that faced accusations of enabling racial profiling, launched in 2011. The company offers neighbors the opportunity to join hyper-local networks specific to their physical community; membership requires submitting a real address. Somewhat quietly, Nextdoor has expanded into one of the largest social networks in the United States. In 2016, the *Verge* estimated that Nextdoor had more than ten million registered users on its network.[9] According to its website, it serves more than 240,000 households in the United States, France, Germany, Australia, and several other countries.[10] Nextdoor has been able to use their scale to broker valuable partnerships with local governments and organizing bodies, as well as authorities like police departments.[11] There's even a widely followed parody Twitter account, @bestofnextdoor, devoted to tweeting the most absurd and entertaining messages that neighbors share.

Compared to Peggy, the moderators of Nextdoor neighborhoods have a lot less visibility and power. "I would like a lot more transparency about who is running these Nextdoors and . . . what their standards are," she said. The Nextdoor website offers some clarity: there are Nextdoor Leads for each neighborhood, locals who "do not work for Nextdoor and are not compensated in any way."[12] Leads can redefine the neighborhood's boundaries, close discussions, and enforce guidelines, but they can't ban someone from the Nextdoor community. They also don't create the rules—Nextdoor has an extensive list of community guidelines that broadly apply to all its communities. These guidelines have a lot in common with some of Peggy's: for example, Nextdoor says it will ban businesses that engage in fraudulent advertising.[13] Another Nextdoor guideline admonishes: "Don't assume someone is suspicious because of their race or ethnicity," which seems obvious, though clearly it isn't.[14] Neighbors who don't like their local Lead can appeal to Nextdoor's leadership. The layered moderation may feel reassuring, since it offers an avenue to oust a troublesome moderator without disbanding the local group. Someone who doesn't like Peggy's LISTSERV, on the other hand, is welcome to argue with her, leave the Cleveland Park LISTSERV, or start their own separate group, but the only authorities above her are the administrators of the Groups.io platform and the actual law. The LISTSERV governance model is not democratic, but that's a trade-off—the moderators' authority and voice may be the very things that have helped the Cleveland Park LISTSERV thrive. Peggy says she appreciates having that level of ownership, even as she wonders how the LISTSERV stacks up against Nextdoor. Reassuringly for Peggy and other local LISTSERV administrators across the country, researchers have found that neighbors haven't adopted Nextdoor at the expense of local LISTSERVs, Facebook groups, or other community media—instead, they've tended to incorporate Nextdoor as one more element in an already-diverse media mix.[15]

The role of neighborhood LISTSERV moderator isn't for the faint of heart or the short of time. It's a full-time job. Local businesses can pay a fee to run an ad in the Cleveland Park LISTSERV, and these fees cover some of the expenses, Peggy says. Now that the LISTSERV has migrated to a more stable platform, Peggy wants to expand advertising. Even with advertising revenue, it's not a lucrative gig, compared to others. But Peggy is one of those people who try to hold the community together— she's participated in the Cleveland Park Historical Society, run for (and won) a seat on DC's neighborhood advisory councils, and served on many neighborhood boards. The LISTSERV is just another way to do the work.

She says she values the personal connections she forms with her neighbors more than almost any other aspect of her job. She's met people on the street who subscribe to the LISTSERV. They've stopped her to tell her how the listserv helped them find their lost cat, get a job, or meet their mate. "They feel like they know me," she said. And she feels like she knows them: when she learned from a mutual friend that one of her frequent posters recently passed away, she "felt like I had lost a friend." She'd never met him in person, but "had been discussing things by email with him" for more than ten years. It may seem funny that a LISTSERV for neighbors was the only place these two neighbors ever interacted, but the LISTSERV brings out people's passions, and, said Peggy, "people are very passionate about where they live."

Enter the TOTs

It's a theme that recurs in a conversation with Juliet Eldred, even though on the surface of it, the group that Juliet administers looks nothing like the Cleveland Park LISTSERV. Whereas members of the Cleveland Park LISTSERV share sincere text-based email messages about lost pets, the members of New Urbanist Memes for Transit-Oriented Teens (yes, that's the real name; it's called NUMTOT for short) swap snarky memes about urban planners and global transit systems. Right now, in the early days of November, Halloween pictures are still straggling in—it's amazing the many creative ways people can find to dress like their most or least favorite subway line.

Juliet started the group in 2017, when she was an overworked college student majoring in geography at the University of Chicago, and she needed to blow off steam. Her method of choice was making inside jokes about famous urban planners of the past. If this seems like a niche activity, it is, but a surprisingly popular one nonetheless. NUMTOT now has more than 170,000 members and has spawned scores of spin-offs, including local chapters, accessibility- and sustainability-focused chapters, and a dating group. It's resonated, Juliet says, with young people who are moving to cities in increasing numbers,[16] majoring in increasingly popular city-related disciplines like urban planning,[17] and (among other things) going carless. It's not exactly a neighborhood group, so much as it is a group *about* neighborhoods. But when asked what makes it special, Juliet says that it's "this interest and desire to make the places we live in better that isn't common to everyone in the group but is common to the group overall." Fittingly, the group has helped some members discover careers in public transportation, Juliet said.

It's also turned Juliet into an unintentional influencer, a mantle that she seems to wear uncomfortably. While some influencers seek the spotlight, posting endless shots of their vacations and outfits to Instagram, Juliet says that as the group's profile has grown, she's tried to draw some boundaries between her role as NUMTOT creator and the rest of her life. This is especially challenging because, in the world of young people who love urban transit policy, having started NUMTOT is quite the laurel. Once, a member went through her private Instagram and liked six years' worth of photos. When she asked about it, the response was "you're the NUMTOT queen." Another time, Juliet popped into the dating spin-off group only to see an awkward thread in which other members talked about what it might be like to date her. She left. People have asked her for photos at conferences. Often, people will send her online messages that feel "overly familiar," she said wryly.

The boundary is especially hard for Juliet to enforce, because she grew up on the internet. She says she met her current boyfriend through Twitter, and when she started at the University of Chicago, she befriended several other students whom she'd originally met online. As a high school student with a passion for music, she established a network through Tumblr. "I've lived multiple lives online," she said. When we spoke, she was twenty-five.

Being a NUMTOT admin has also had positive influences on her life. In mid-to-late 2018, the TOTs started getting a lot of publicity. The *New York Times* wrote a story about the group and its relationship with its spin-offs, right around the same time the *Guardian* also profiled them. Juliet started to get questions about her Facebook hobby from higher-ups at the company where she worked.

"I had to explain what shitposting was at lunch, and that was uncomfortable for everybody," she said. The upside is that she put NUMTOT on her resume when interviewing for her next job, and she found people were interested in hearing about it. "The social capital of the group put my resume up a couple notches," she said. Researchers who study social networks define social capital as "the aggregate value of social interactions and structure," and have suggested that having high social capital can help with tasks like finding a job. Sharing messages and memes on platforms like Facebook can help communities generate social capital.[18] While the group may have helped Juliet get her job, the downside is that she now has to be more thoughtful about what she posts and how she moderates the group, since her boss and coworkers might be in it.

As Juliet's grown up, so has the group. The *New York Times* article talks about the ways in which the group has splintered as it's scaled, with discussions getting bogged down between factions.[19] These are some of the challenges of scale—groups grow, they get influxes of new members, and their culture shifts and hopefully adapts. As the group has grown, so has the size, number, and popularity of its spin-offs. Juliet says that many of these spin-offs aren't officially associated with NUMTOT, and she herself usually doesn't participate in them except as the occasional lurker. In the case of the dating spin-off—appropriately called NUMTinder—she specifically asked the moderators to mention in the description that the group wasn't formally associated with the NUMTOT admins.

"Those groups have created a parallel ecosystem that feels a little bit more like the group felt at the beginning," she said. Members of the groups agree. Ryan Hardy has been a member of the big NUMTOT group since mid-2018. He says he comments on posts three to ten times a week, and occasionally creates and shares detailed transit-oriented data visualizations that attract scores of comments.

"My first impression was local politics was a nice refuge from the quagmire of national politics, so when I initially joined the group, I saw people who supported what I wanted," he said. "As time went on I think discussions got increasingly contentious, and I felt some of the bitterness of national politics creep back." He started joining local spin-offs. First he moved to Pasadena, California, and joined Angelic Thoughts for SoCal TOTs, a spin-off for Los Angeles–based TOTs. He moved to Boulder, Colorado, and joined a group for Denver-area TOTs. Finally, he moved to DC, and joined 7000-Series Memes for Congressionally Disenfranchised Teens—the DC spin-off. The group's name is a complex inside reference: the "7000-Series" is a name for a new line of DC Metro trains; "Congressionally Disenfranchised" is less a joke than DC's long-running reality.

Ryan says there's a cultural difference between the spin-offs and the parent group. "The discussions are a bit more productive [in the spin-offs]. You might see a CTA [call to action] that actually results in something," he said. "The discussions are more neighbor-to-neighbor, even though you might live an hour from the person you're talking to." He says the local groups have also inspired him to take an active interest in his city: "NUMTOT did inspire me to visit and participate in city meetings and transportation planning open houses in Boulder . . . I already had an interest in the topic, which is why I joined, but joining the group amplified that interest and made me eager to participate in the process." Local calls to action are less common in the main NUMTOT group, which isn't as focused on specific community action.

Thomas Andrew Nimmo started 7000-Series Memes for Congressionally Disenfranchised Teens in late 2017. He sometimes posts about active ways to make the city better, but "most people who do participate are just participating in it for making jokes about the Metro." The Metro, of course, is DC's public train system—where, Tom says, one NUMTOT once reported finding a live lobster wandering about. The group also does regular happy hours and meetups, not exclusively about trains. They now have a little more than four thousand members, buoyed in part by student populations at nearby Georgetown and George Washington Universities. The group has a limited relationship with its larger parent, although sometimes, Tom says, discussions will migrate from the larger group to the smaller one. He says that on a typical day he spends as little as ten minutes on moderation, but he can never entirely step away. He still remembers logging in from a friend's destination wedding in Scotland to lock comments on a particularly quarrelsome thread.

Juliet has also been outspoken about the challenges of moderation work—she told the *New York Times* it felt like she was "dealing with what I call my one hundred thousand large adult children."[20] Perhaps this is why the official NUMTOT guidelines sound like they were written by someone at the tail end of a long day. Consider this one, which explains one of the reasons mods might not approve a post: "We've all had shitty commutes; no one cares." Or this one, intended for members who complain that not approving their posts is a violation of free speech: "This is a private group, and we don't owe you anything."

Each of these rules represents a hard-won lesson, something I heard from Peggy as well. Every rule has a reason, or came out of some crisis that moderators had to handle. While Peggy turned to advertising to help pay the LISTSERV's costs, Juliet suggested another option—tipping the moderators. The idea did not go down easily at first.

"She got dragged by a bunch of people for using the term 'emotional labor,'" said Tom. "While I'm not sure how I felt about ascribing the same thing to what I'm doing in my group, I could see how it is emotional labor for her and some of the other people in the bigger group."

Emotional labor is an academic concept that's moved into the popular realm; it occurs when workers must suppress their own emotions as part of stimulating emotions, either positive or negative, in others (usually, customers). A key example, cited by sociologist Arlie Hochschild when she defined the term in the early 1980s, would be flight attendants, who have to manage their gestures, words, tone, and even facial expressions to make customers feel welcome. Social media didn't exist when Hochschild wrote her book, but other scholars have started studying emotional labor in online comments. A study of Reddit moderators, in 2019, opens with the following:

> Moderators are taxed with the emotional labor involved in generating and enforcing shared norms with respect to how Redditors should interact with each other.[21]

Academics refer to it as "enforcing shared norms"; Tom thinks of it as handling the "drama" that arises in the group. Now, of course, there are ways to compensate people for that work—the NUMTOT admin/mod team have added a digital tip jar, through a service called Ko-fi. Juliet says she got the idea from a Facebook group for people who moderate Facebook groups (meta, but helpful!). She'll collect $150 to $200 at a time and then divide it up among the twelve-member mod and admin team. Compared to working a professional job, tips come out to pennies per hour. But it's a valuable gesture. Many community moderators "do not feel fully appreciated by members of their subreddits, which may negatively affect the recruitment and retention of moderation teams," according to the same researchers who made the point about emotional labor.[22] Or, as Tom puts it, offering people a mod job is basically asking "Would you like some more responsibility, with no payoff?"

The big NUMTOT group has warmed to the tip jar over time.

Ryan, the DC NUMTOT and data visualizer mentioned above, says he's donated.

The tip jar is not Juliet's only income-generating suggestion.

"I think Facebook should pay us," she said. "Most of our members are between 18 and 34 and people have told me that this group is the one thing that has kept them from deactivating their Facebook." Although she warns that the plural of anecdote is not data, she believes she and other admins are "providing a service of value to [Facebook]."

She's not wrong about the value of her work to Facebook, but if the history of the internet is any predictor, it seems unlikely that Facebook is suddenly going to start sharing its revenue with its many community moderators. After all, the question has been around almost as long as the internet itself. In the early 1990s, according to an article in *Wired*, people paid for internet access by the hour, and services like chat rooms and forums accounted for many hours spent online. A dedicated corps of community volunteers, often recruited because they were especially active users already, offered to moderate AOL chat rooms in exchange for free hours. By 1996, according to an estimate in the same *Wired* article, AOL was earning $7 million a month, with the help of thirty-three thousand volunteers.[23] Then AOL switched to charging a monthly flat fee for internet access. Suddenly, instead of free hours, community volunteers—called Community Leaders—got at most an occasional discount. Many left, but others kept on volunteering, despite the three-month training program and the lack of real compensation. In 1999, seven former Community Leaders filed a suit with the Department of Labor, suggesting that AOL owed them back wages for their unpaid time. Two of them filed a complaint against AOL in federal court, opening up a class action lawsuit that dragged on until 2010, when AOL settled it for an eye-popping $15 million.

The idea of volunteer online labor—a novelty in AOL's early days—has become a backbone of the digital economy, which makes it hard to legislate who is owed money for what. In an article in *Priceonomics*, writer Alex Mayyasi says:

> When separating valid volunteerism from illegal unpaid labor, one criterion considered by the Department of Labor is whether the work displaces a regular employee. But if you substitute *user* for *volunteer*, "displacing regular employees" pretty much defines the business model of a number of digital companies.[24]

Mayyasi mentions Wikimedia, which he says became a nonprofit in part because it was built by volunteers who "would revolt if banner ads one day appeared," and Reddit. Reddit offers moderators a lot more leeway than AOL offered its Community Leaders, but that didn't stop a consortium of Reddit moderators from going on strike in 2015. The strike shut down many popular forums and came to be known as the Reddit Blackout. The immediate cause was that the company fired a community liaison employee without giving moderators any notice, but the reasons went deeper than that, as Brian Lynch and Courtnie Swearingen, two moderators who led the shutdown, explained in an op-ed in the *New York Times*:

The issue goes beyond Reddit. We are concerned with what a move like this means for for-profit companies that depend on the free labor of volunteers—and whether they truly understand what makes an online community vibrant.[25]

The moderators weren't demanding to be paid a salary: "We donate our time and talents to Reddit, a for-profit company, because we truly like building cool things on the internet for others to enjoy." They may have accepted—even embraced—their volunteer status, but they were asking for something equally significant: an acknowledgment that Reddit values the moderators who keep the site going.

A similar controversy erupted at *HuffPost* when the founders sold the site for $315 million in 2011. Some of the writers who'd written for the site for free suggested that unpaid contributors had helped build the organization and should get a cut of the payout.[26] Where did they organize their collective action? A Facebook group. Who bought *HuffPost*? AOL.

For Facebook, there's the added awkwardness of the fact that they already do pay moderators—just not ones like Juliet. The company pays thousands of content moderators, who are responsible for viewing and scrubbing things like child pornography and extreme violence. It turns out machines can do some of the work of identifying this material, but humans need to sign off. Many content moderators are contract employees with professional services firms.[27] Other Facebook users never know content moderators' names, much less the specifics of the work. In one especially harrowing investigation by the *Verge* in 2019, a journalist visited one of these contract content moderation sites. The site sparkled when he showed up for a tour, but employees described a usually filthy workplace, fourteen-page nondisclosure agreements, and a schedule so exacting that they had to use a browser extension to log every time they went to the bathroom. The pay? Fifteen dollars an hour, but in exchange for watching videos of people committing atrocities so horrifying that some employees reported having nightmares about it even after leaving the job.[28,29]

In May 2020, under legal and public pressure, Facebook agreed to pay $52 million to more than ten thousand of these current and former contract moderators. The settlement—which entitles American contractors to at least $1,000 each, and possibly more to cover mental health treatments—may be a landmark move for Facebook, but there are many questions it leaves unanswered. What is a fair wage for moderation? How do companies address the mental toll of this difficult role? And what about community moderators like Juliet, who aren't covered by this type of agreement but find themselves at the intersection of personal and professional use of the platform?

Community moderators enjoy a fair bit of visibility and autonomy on Facebook. It's unclear whether the terms and structure of formal employment with Facebook would be attractive or equitable, considering the way that Facebook and similar companies have treated moderation work, both paid and unpaid. Community may be valuable, but unpaid or lowly paid work is one of the things that has helped it scale.

In Juliet's case, the value creation goes both ways: the social capital she generated as a NUMTOT founder translated into actual financial capital. But not all moderators are so lucky, and one of the fundamental challenges of volunteer-built online communities is whether and how they continue when unpaid moderators run out of time or energy. Juliet says she's proposed archiving the group—i.e., making it inactive—more than once, but other members of the moderation team (including her cofounder) want to keep it open.

Sister Circle

Juliet and Peggy aren't the only ones wondering how to make their moderation hobby pay. Christi Ketchum often finds herself asking the same question. Today, Christi moderates the Sacramento Sister Circle, a 7,700-member strong Facebook community for Black women in Sacramento, California.

Christi started the first Sacramento Sister Circle in 1998 after moving back to Sacramento, her hometown, after college. She read an article in *Essence* magazine about sister circles, groups of black women who provided each other with support and advice, and realized that was what she was missing. Her first sister circle was a group of women who met regularly in person. The group went on hiatus when she moved. In 2010, she returned to Sacramento, and the group really got off the ground. She gathered a group of her friends and family in her living room, and proposed reopening the Sacramento Sister Circle with an online component. She outlined six key goals, which she described to me:

The study of Black women and dismantling stereotypes, mentoring younger women and girls, expanding our horizons and pushing ourselves to get out of our comfort zone, being politically active, being financially aware and independent, being our whole and complete selves spiritually and emotionally.

She says her friends' immediate reaction was "yes yes yes." They started it as a Facebook page, but quickly switched over to a Facebook group, which they saw as more interactive. The only criteria for membership was being a Black woman over the age of eighteen in Sacramento.

When Christi and I spoke, the group had just passed its eighth anniversary. The Facebook group has a governing board of ten people, although Christi says she handles most of the daily moderation herself. Three other admins post articles and information, and handle friend requests to the group. The six pillars, described on the website, are health and wellness, study, financial independence, mentorship, fun and joy, and political engagement.

Since it started, Christi says, the group has served as a unique and valuable online gathering place for the black community in the area, providing space for political involvement and the discussion of issues and events that are "culturally specific to black people."

Recently, for example, the producers of a mainstream movie about Harriet Tubman got into a public disagreement with Girl-Trek, an advocacy movement for black women, with whom they'd been organizing a partnership. The members of Sister Circle had a long discussion about the disagreement, and whether or not they wanted to continue to support the movie.

Members have also come together to advocate within their physical community. In 2016, a member posted in the Facebook group that she'd been called a racial slur by an employee at a local nightclub. Other members started sharing similar stories of discrimination, all taking place at establishments owned by the same company. The admins and members of Sister Circle organized a boycott of that company's properties, and also put out a list of demands that included cultural sensitivity training for the company staff and publishing a dress code so that visitors had an objective standard for turning people away. Within months, Christi says, the company met their demands.

The group also lends its energies to other Black women–supported causes and organizations. They publish voter guides for upcoming elections and have participated in organizing the Black Women's March, a response to the Women's March. This year's Sacramento Black Women's March drew eight hundred attendees, according to an article in the *Sacramento Bee.*[30]

The group also covers difficult conversations about issues like colorism and police brutality. Conversations about colorism, Christi says, have run into hundreds of comments, and she's had to turn comments off because the conversations weren't going in a positive direction. Discussions about the death of Stephon Clark, an unarmed black man who was shot by police in his grandmother's backyard in Sacramento, required special sensitivity, Christi says, because members of the Facebook group had known and loved him.[31] At the same time, the forum provided a safe place for members to talk about Clark's wrongful death and the issues raised by some of his tweets about Black women.[32] "It was a hard conversation and it was a needed conversation," she said. "I don't think we can actually get on the same page until we are all comfortable to talk about where we stand."

Her role in these conversations is to reinforce the rules, make sure there's "no name-calling," and that people are courteous and respectful (two things that her group guidelines stipulate). She spends anywhere from thirty to forty hours a week on moderating the group, and has thought about launching a membership model that would help defray some of the costs. She's not sure what that membership would include, since she'd want it to be something additional to what group members currently get for free. She's also thought about migrating off Facebook, in light of the platform's current troubles. She wonders "What happens if something happens to Facebook—do we just lose everything?" A universe without Facebook may seem improbable, but the story of the Cleveland Park LISTSERV demonstrates that technology companies can change their strategies anytime—without notice.

Unlike Juliet, Christi doesn't dream of archiving or deactivating the group. She's a community activist to her core—she's worked in leadership development for a foster youth organization, and in advocacy around child welfare and crime. Especially when Sacramento Sister Circle moves into more offline activism, she says that being the moderator of it "puts me in a unique position to have an influence." It's time-consuming, but good community-building often is. And, as everyone I spoke to knows, good moderators are hard to find. "I always think of myself as a bridge-builder and someone who naturally brings people together," she said. "That's definitely a quality not everybody has."

Bringing the Revolution

Sleeping Giants and the
Battle over Online Advertising

I t began with an almost perfect irony. A company that builds hiring tools saw that one of their ads had appeared on the conservative news website Breitbart, above the headline "There's No Hiring Bias Against Women In Tech, They Just Suck at Interviews." On November 27, 2016, a Twitter user tweeted a screenshot at Workable, the company that had paid to place the ad.

Workable CEO Nikos Moraitakis replied the same day:

Nikos Moraitakis @moraitakis · Nov 27, 2016

> thanks for the note. We didn't choose to advertise there (part of the google network). We are adding it to our opt out list now

Moraitakis later told the *New York Times* that he "nearly had a heart attack" when he saw his company's ad running above that particular Breitbart headline.[1] Like a lot of companies—and even governments—Workable had gotten tripped up in the shadowy world of programmatic advertising. A description of how programmatic advertising operates, from a 2019 academic paper by the media researchers Joshua A. Braun, John D. Coakley, and Emily West, illustrates how complicated it is:

> While programmatic advertising can take a number of forms, most commonly it consists of an online auction that occurs each time a web page is loaded, in which a publisher puts up ad space for sale along with details on the user about to view it. Advertisers bid on the attention of the user based on their perceived desirability as a customer. Intermediaries known as ad-tech firms handle the details of each transaction. These intermediaries are numerous (though they are often owned by the same tech giants), and it is not uncommon for a single transaction to involve four or more ad-tech companies. The resulting complexity of each transaction, combined with the fact that programmatic advertising tends to focus advertisers' attention on reaching desirable users at the expense of editorial context, has meant that until recently advertisers were often unaware of where on the web their ads were appearing.[2]

Over the past several years, programmatic advertising has become a key part of many publishers' revenue mix. The trade publication *eMarketer* predicted that US advertisers would spend $60 billion on programmatic display advertising in 2019, and that by 2021, almost 88 percent of all US digital-display ad dollars would be programmatic.[3] Also in 2019, the European branch of the Interactive Advertising Bureau, an industry body dedicated to all forms of digital advertising, predicted that "programmatic will be the driving force behind all future digital advertising growth."[4] Programmatic revenues depend on pageviews, which leaves the system open to exploitation by shady niche publishers looking to make a quick buck. The researchers noted that programmatic advertising has "been readily exploited by proprietors of clickbait sites who spin up viral content featuring miracle diets, strange cosmetic trends, and hoax news articles solely for the purpose of generating a profit."[5] In more recent years, governments have also scrutinized possible links between programmatic advertising and funding terrorism.

In November 2016, inspired in part by the 2016 presidential election, two marketers began an online campaign to raise public awareness of how programmatic advertising operates. The loose citizen collective calls itself Sleeping Giants. Its tagline is "to make bigotry and sexism less profitable," which is a lot catchier than "to shed light on the labyrinthine workings of programmatic advertising." They visit far-right publishers' websites, take screenshots of the advertisements that appear, and tweet the screenshots at companies in an attempt to pressure them to block these sites from their advertising mix. The founders say the goal is partly educational—in a programmatic deal, advertisers don't deal with sites directly, and so they often don't know where their ads are running. Sleeping Giants' first campaign—and a focus of their work even now—began with tweeting at programmatic advertisers whose ads appeared on Breitbart. Sleeping Giants has since expanded to targeting advertisers on right-leaning TV programs and petitioning tech companies to shut down the accounts of known racist ideologues. By one estimate, they managed to help cut the number of advertisers on Breitbart by 90 percent in just two months, from March to May 2017.[6]

Nandini Jammi, thirty-one years old, cofounded Sleeping Giants. She was living in Berlin during the 2016 presidential election. She visited Breitbart's site for the first time after Trump won. Over the course of the 2016 election, she'd watched as Breitbart had become a formidable power in conservative circles, "driving the agenda of partisan conservative outlets across the web."[7] Steve Bannon, former executive chairman of Breitbart and one of the chief architects of the site's rise, had just gotten a plum job as chief strategist in Trump's administration. It was also suggested—especially by the left—that Bannon was the driving force behind Breitbart's increasingly hard-line views on immigration and economic policy.[8,9] Notably, he had drawn praise from Richard Spencer, the avowed white nationalist leader.[10] Nandini's political views skewed left, but she wanted to better understand a site that suddenly seemed to be driving the national conversation. How did the site run? What did it cover? And, most important, who supported it?

An ad copywriter, Nandini immediately noticed the mainstream advertisements all over the right-leaning site. She says she saw ads for companies like Old Navy, where she shops. She knew that these ads were being chosen specifically for her through programmatic ad auctions. This also meant that companies she did business with were either intentionally or unknowingly helping to keep Breitbart in business.

"My immediate conclusion was that there's no way they [the companies placing the ads] know, because I'm being retargeted across the web," she said. She saw one ad—jarring, she says, in context—that featured a mixed-race family.

Top editors at Breitbart say the site's content isn't racist or sexist, though they are proudly conservative and overall pro-Trump. But the site's editorial decision-making has drawn criticism from several quarters. The *New York Times* described Breitbart's editorial philosophy as one driven by rumor and right-wing conspiracy:

> The site refers to "migrant rape gangs" in Europe, and was among the first news outlets to disseminate unsubstantiated rumors that Mrs. Clinton was in ill health. Its writers often vilify the Black Lives Matter movement, emphasizing what they call a scourge of "black-on-black crime," and described "young Muslims in the West" as the world's "ticking time bomb."[11]

The Breitbart reader community is often willing to go where the writers won't. On a recent article about Chick-fil-A, the fast food chain known for its owners' opposition to same-sex marriage, commenters note that homosexuality is a sin, refer to gay people in disparaging terms, and call the gay rights movement a "Rainbow reich."[12] Although Breitbart editors claim to be tough on hate speech, critics say far too many comments slip through the cracks.[13] At a time when many organizations have done away with comment sections precisely to avoid these types of discussions, the leadership at Breitbart seems to invite them.

After visiting the site, Nandini wrote a *Medium* post for her fellow marketing professionals, urging them to block their company's advertising from appearing on Breitbart. Although programmatic advertisers don't always know which sites their ads will end up on, they can "blacklist" certain sites, which means their ads will never appear there. That's what Nandini encouraged even low- to mid-level marketers to do. She titled her post with a call to action: "PPC [Pay-Per-Click] Marketers: Don't Wait for Permission to Blacklist Breitbart News."[14] She linked to a help desk article that explained the blacklisting process in easy terms. She published the article on November 23, 2016, and . . . crickets. "It wasn't a very sexy thing to talk about," Nandini said. But the post did catch the attention of Matt Rivitz, who'd recently started the anonymous Twitter account Sleeping Giants. Rivitz, in his late forties, was also an ad executive, although he'd cut his teeth on TV advertisements. He had a similarly surreal experience browsing Breitbart for the first time: "I was completely blown away by what I saw," he said. He says he still remembers one particularly controversial video article in which participants were asked whether they'd rather their children had feminism or cancer.[15,16] The video is no longer available on the site, but descriptions of it exist elsewhere online. Most TV advertising is direct, not programmatic, and he didn't know how programmatic advertising worked. His first reaction when he saw mainstream ads running on Breitbart was astonishment. He had almost no Twitter presence: "I had a personal Twitter handle and I'd sent maybe twelve tweets in my time on Twitter," he said. But Twitter was "public and people can see it," so he started taking screenshots of advertisements on Breitbart and sending them to the advertisers in question. That was how he learned how murky online ad exchanges are. "I thought I was sitting on a *60 Minutes* story," he said. "Why the hell don't these companies know where their ads are running?"

Part of Sleeping Giants' success, as Braun and company note, is the way they've distilled a complex problem into a single slogan and a series of easy steps. Programmatic advertising is complicated, but rather than endlessly explaining its intricacies, Matt and Nandini focus on its consequences and what people can do. Sleeping Giants' founders now jointly run a Twitter and Facebook community. Their Twitter account has (as of this writing) nearly 250,000 followers. On Facebook, they have 67,392 followers. It's by tapping into this community that they've been able to succeed. They say anyone can be a "Giant." There's a three-step process outlined at the top of the Sleeping Giants Twitter feed:

Sleeping Giants ✔️
@slpng_giants

HOW TO BE A GIANT:
1. GO to Breitbart and take a screenshot of an ad next to some of their content.
2. TWEET the screenshot to the company with a polite, non-offensive note to notify them of the placement.
3. TAG @slpng_giants so we can keep track of the progress.

They've expanded the focus from Breitbart to other right-leaning sites, politicians, and causes, and inspired Sleeping Giants chapters in other countries. They estimate they've prompted more than four thousand advertisers—including many recognizable names—to blacklist Breitbart.[17] Matt and Nandini have also been profiled in the *New York Times*, and in 2019, Sleeping Giants won a Cannes Lion—one of the advertising industry's highest honors.[18]

In the *New York Times* article mentioned above, a Breitbart spokesman referred to Sleeping Giants' tactics as "speech suppression through economic force," and on the site, a Breitbart writer called it "harassment against advertisers."[19] Nandini doesn't see any conflict between Sleeping Giants' work and free speech: "You're free to say whatever you want to say, but you don't have a right to advertising."

Still, targeting advertisers is an activist technique that's historically been associated more with conservatives than liberals, according to researchers. "In the 1980s and 1990s [activists] became well-known for protesting content on the basis usually of its depictions of sex and sexuality," write Braun, Coakley, and West in their paper. In October 2014, the right-leaning #GamerGate movement pressured advertisers to stop running campaigns with publishers who carried stories attacking traditional gamer identity. Breitbart's then tech editor Milo Yiannopoulos wrote a couple of articles praising the #GamerGate movement and supporting their tactics.[20]

Matt and Nandini don't actively take sides; they both repeatedly say that their campaign isn't about politics. "Hate speech is not a legitimate point of view," Nandini told me. But Sleeping Giants' work is certainly pegged to power, particularly the increasing influence of right-wing officials in the Trump administration. The Sleeping Giants slogan, although ostensibly apolitical, has helped attract and, according to Nandini, empower many people who felt dissatisfied after the election. "People started to [send tweets], and advertisers would peel off at a rate of ten to twenty a day," Matt says. "That's how it started to grow."

Breitbart has hit back. One of Sleeping Giants' first big campaigns, right after the election, was Kellogg's. In response to a message from Sleeping Giants, Kellogg's decided to drop the site. Breitbart responded by encouraging readers to boycott Kellogg's cereal, referring to the Kellogg's move as an "an escalation in the war by leftist companies . . . against conservative customers whose values propelled Donald Trump into the White House."[21]

Sleeping Giants' cause got an indirect boost in early to mid-2017 when investigations by news outlets revealed that money from several large advertisers—including the British government—might have ended up on YouTube videos promoting violent terrorism.[22] It was the same system—programmatic advertising—that Sleeping Giants had been criticizing for several months. The scandal spread from the UK to the United States, as major advertisers like Walmart and Starbucks suspended advertising on YouTube pending further investigation.[23] When Nandini mentioned that Google was summoned to a hearing by British lawmakers to explain how it happened, her voice crackled with righteous satisfaction: "It's big for a big company or an agency to say we are going to pause advertising with

Google or Facebook. I was like, now it's all going to change," she said. The satisfaction quickly gave way to resignation: "That was so naïve."

Google's UK managing director issued a statement acknowledging "we don't always get it right" with online advertising, while also emphasizing that the offensive ad displays were limited to a small fraction of YouTube's overall content.[24] A few days later, Google announced changes, including "taking a tougher stance on hateful, offensive and derogatory content" and controls that would make it easier for advertisers to restrict *all* their advertising from appearing on certain types of videos (previously, these controls had existed at the level of each individual ad campaign).[25] While these moves might have represented real changes for Google, for Nandini, they didn't go far enough. "Brands kept telling us that they had blacklisted Breitbart, but they were still appearing on Breitbart. So we were like, what's up with your technology?" Both Matt and Nandini say they've tried reaching out to Google and Facebook, two of the largest tech companies involved in ad placements, to get them to remove Breitbart from ad exchanges altogether. But the tech companies didn't respond to the same tactics that individual advertisers did. So Nandini and Matt refined their strategy. Instead of just pinging the companies on Twitter, they started looking up executives' email addresses. Their first such campaign targeted a senior-level marketing executive at Facebook. Nandini's justification: "It's her job to make sure that brands are safe; she's not doing her job." She put the executive's picture and job title on the Facebook page, as well as a templated email that Facebook community members could copy, fill out, and send. Her goal in putting up a template was twofold: "One, people won't do it unless you give them a template. Two, to guide and lead on the tone that we wanted to take. We didn't want people to send hateful messages; we wanted them to send informed and assertive messages." She says the executive probably received "dozens of emails" from members of the Sleeping Giants community. She knows that because community shares are the lifeblood of Sleeping Giants' work. Whenever a community member tweets or sends an email, they're encouraged to share their message and the response (if any) with the rest of the community. To Nandini's surprise, the executive responded, although it was only to confirm that Breitbart did not qualify as hate speech under Facebook's then standards. It was not what Sleeping Giants had hoped for, but it was better than the nothing they'd gotten from the platforms before. "I was like, 'We have something interesting on our hands. [Writing to individual] people gets responses.'" They intensified the letter-writing campaign against that particular executive, but Nandini also began to look for other individuals they could target at tech companies, advertisers, and elsewhere. "It's usually like the VP of marketing, CMO. Sometimes the CEO, but usually it's someone a little bit below that," she said. "It's incredible to see how quickly things move after we email the right person."

She says that targeting individuals has been "one of the most effective tactics ever." She also realized that this was an ideal use for the Facebook community. While Twitter was rapid-fire and fast-moving, Facebook provided a home for longer-duration campaigns, featuring multiple rounds of emails and responses, and templates for individual emails. "We were able to stay on a particular topic or company because we had Facebook." The Facebook and Twitter communities also differ in age and tolerance. The Facebook community skews older—"Moms and grandmas," in Nandini's terms. In the past, when she's posted messages on Facebook that used profanity, she got responses from community members asking her to watch her language. They've used Facebook to target executives at Apple (requesting they drop Telegram, a messaging app that white nationalists used to circulate lists of Jewish users); GitHub (the software company, over its contracts with US Immigration and Customs Enforcement); and the International Fact-Checking Network (asking them to explain why they certified the conservative *Daily Caller*'s fact-checking unit). The bulk of their fury is still reserved for the platforms that run ad exchanges and app stores: the Facebooks, Googles, and Apples of the world, who have enormous power and yet, according to Sleeping Giants, continue to work with white nationalist publishers. Many of Sleeping Giants' Facebook posts—an irony they readily admit—take aim at the company:

Sleeping Giants
October 17 · 🌐

Mark Zuckerberg bravely defended his inalienable right to make billions of dollars monetizing fake news, hate speech and everything in between.

In late 2019, Sleeping Giants tried to take out a Facebook ad that targeted Facebook employees, encouraging them to question their management as to why Facebook had designated Breitbart News Network as a "trusted" news source.

The campaign is ongoing, encouraging individuals to take action, often against the same powerful corporations that they work for or use. It's the same rallying cry that Nandini issued in her first *Medium* post, and it's been part of Sleeping Giants' DNA ever since.

Matt, who handles more of Twitter, has adapted the "approaching individuals" tactic to that platform: "Here's a list of the public Twitter handles of the people on the board of a certain place." Targeting individuals and hunting down their email addresses is rightfully controversial. It's been used by online mobs to target and harass private figures. Matt reflects on the parallel, saying the information they share is "always public, never private. Business and personal shouldn't really cross, so that's hopefully all in good faith."

Some media scholars dispute whether Twitter networks qualify as a community, in part because many members of a network spend time "lurking or intermittently tweeting" rather than actively participating.[26] But Nandini refers to the work she does, sometimes for as long as eight hours a day, although usually less, as community management. Matt agrees that what they've created at Sleeping Giants is a community, which he defines:

> I think it's a shared set of values and principles, and a
> shared mission and ethics, and also just the ability to

communicate with each other and share ideas, and that's what makes any community.

As they've grown, they've involved the community in decision-making. Matt says they'll often ask community members who their next target should be, or if a particular action seems in keeping with the mission. In addition to Breitbart, Sleeping Giants has gone after advertisers on Bill O'Reilly's show, after the TV host was accused of sexual harassment, and on Laura Ingraham's show, after she mocked a survivor of the Parkland school shooting. They also pressured social networks to drop Far Right personality Alex Jones.

Sleeping Giants ✔
@slpng_giants

Hey @instagram.

Alex Jones of Infowars, who is currently being sued by Sandy Hook families for exactly this hoax, is still on your platform.

Just thought you should know who you're amplifying.

A Sleeping Giants Twitter post about Alex Jones,
demonstrating how Sleeping Giants pressures platforms.

All of these targets faced consequences—O'Reilly is no longer with Fox, Ingraham took a hiatus, and Alex Jones was permanently suspended by Twitter, and several services stopped carrying his podcast.[27] In many cases, other social pressures combined with Sleeping Giants' work in order to achieve these outcomes. Nevertheless, Sleeping Giants has been uniquely effective in galvanizing public interest around a complicated and not particularly sexy issue. Eleven Sleeping Giants chapters have sprung up in other countries, although not all of these chapters are currently operating. The French and Australian outposts, however, are, and Nandini says they're two of their most active. Rachel[28] is one of two coordinators for the Sleeping Giants account in France. I spoke to Rachel as she was wrapping up a rough month. She estimated she'd given sixty media interviews over the past four weeks. Rachel is anonymous—the name Rachel is a "family name" but a pseudonym, and she asked me not to reveal too many details of her past professional life, because they're unusual enough to identify her.

Sleeping Giants France started by targeting Breitbart when it announced a European expansion, but have since expanded significantly. They ran a lengthy campaign against advertisers on the French far-right publication *Boulevard Voltaire*, conducted another against a TV station that wanted to give a far-right journalist a regular show, and, in 2017, participated in a joint effort to financially de-platform a crowdfunded boat that aimed to hamper refugee-assistance efforts in the Mediterranean. This last in particular serves as an example "of how a chapter adapted Sleeping Giants' basic tactics to its local context," write Braun, Coakley, and West.[29] Rachel says the French chapter is "very scientific in our approach and extremely rigorous" about research. They can spend half a day arguing about the intricacies of wording, in part because even a minor mistake can discredit them. In addition to inspecting *Boulevard Voltaire*'s source code to learn which advertising the site runs, they find and contact the companies that host far-right websites. They've also built a wide network of people who reach out to companies via email and Facebook, because many French brands aren't on Twitter.

One of the interesting things about Sleeping Giants is that it's turned people who don't like social media into extremely active social media users. Rachel says she "hates" Facebook—its reach, its impunity—but uses it extensively nevertheless. Rachel sees their work as stemming a global "normalization of hatred": "People say what they would have said only to allies in a very closed circle ten years ago. Now they write it on Twitter or on Facebook or on the media," she says. This trend worries her. Her past work took her all over the world, including to conflict zones, and she draws a direct link between intolerant speech and intolerant actions: "The new form of ethnically or racially motivated terrorism . . . is not a freak occurrence. It's the result of what people have tolerated for too long a time." This is the French mentality, which is why inciting racial hatred is a crime in France. More than one of Sleeping Giants France's targets have been convicted of it. The most frustrating part of the task, Rachel says, is that they're "doing something that should not need to be done." Politicians and tech companies, she says, have the power and resources to take up these tasks but don't, which is why individual volunteers have had to act. For Matt and Nandini, Sleeping Giants succeeded because it gave individuals an enormous amount of power at a time when traditional methods of political involvement felt remote or ineffective: "This was not like calling your congressman and waiting for a couple months for something to happen. They could be like I sent that message and I got a response back. And it made people feel really powerful at a time when we felt powerless," Nandini said.

She is also quick to point out that Sleeping Giants is not one-sided. They engage in legitimate dissent, although she struggles to define the term exactly. A message along the lines of "your campaign is stupid, why are you doing it?" might qualify as le-gitimate dissent, but name-calling won't. She remembers one Facebook exchange with a vehement critic. She replied to his ini-tial angry sally with "How are you doing, are you having a bad day?" The tone shifted. While he didn't thank her, he did back off. "Maybe they're just itching to get into a fight, and we don't give it to them," she said. At least, not that kind of fight. But reading mean messages for a chunk of the day can get wearying, right? Not necessarily. "I don't feel anything," she said. "It's not personal."

It's definitely personal for Matt. When Sleeping Giants started out, he and Nandini made a deliberate choice to stay anony-mous. They both work in advertising, and Matt was concerned for his family. He's Jewish, which adds another level of risk in some of the far-right outlets Sleeping Giants has targeted. In July 2018, the conservative outlet the *Daily Caller* published Matt's name without his permission. Diligent site commenters uncovered his home address and posted it in the comments section of the arti-cle, as well as information about his family, neighborhood, and educational background. What followed next was "one of the worst months of my life," he said. He described it:

It was exactly what I feared. My family and I, my son got death threats online—he was fourteen at the time. My wife got all these calls on her personal phone, our address was on Daily Stormer, Breitbart, it was really, really, really bad.

"Once he went public, that was like the face of the Jewish conspiracy [to critics]," said Nandini. For better or worse, Matt's face became publicly associated with the campaign, especially for detractors.

Sleeping Giants Exposed
@ExposedGiants

> Matt Rivitz & his "Sleeping Giants" have harassed thousands of businesses to chill speech. Learn how to stop them here. Not affiliated with Matt Rivitz.

An anti–Sleeping Giants Twitter account,
featuring a doctored image of Matt as its avatar.

In the hours after his identity was revealed, he says he decided to accept the publicity. "My calculus was 'I can either run away from that, or run at it and own what this thing is,' and for better or worse, I did that," he said. He acknowledged the doxxing on Twitter, admitted that he was one of the founders of Sleeping Giants, and agreed to do interviews. Of the decision, he said, "There's great power in that."

Sleeping Giants ✅ @slpng_giants · Jul 17, 2018

Hey everyone. It's Matt Rivitz. Founder of Sleeping Giants here. Last night, @peterjhasson from @dailycaller decided to publish my name as well as the names of my family & friends. And, curiously, a tweet I wrote to Ikea customer service. Which is weird.

While this isn't obviously how I wanted things to play out, I have nothing to hide. I am super proud of what we've built here and the fact that there are now hundreds of thousands of people across the world who have joined together to make hate unprofitable.

This has never been about me or us. It's about you. Thanks for your support. The mission continues. I, and the rest of the team here, have always wanted to stay anonymous to keep this about the mission rather than the individuals involved. That hasn't changed.

Now back to being called fascist communist soros-funded free speech-stomping anti-American deep state plants like we always have.

Four tweets Matt sent from the Sleeping Giants
handle after his identity was revealed.

He received a completely unexpected—to him, anyway—outpouring of support from the community. "Kind of out of nowhere, everyone started to do this 'I am Spartacus' thing, 'I am sleeping giants' all day. There were thousands of tweets like that, that really blew my mind," he said. "I still kind of get chills about that. You try to foster a community where people are there for each other. That was the best moment of this community because I felt very singled out and very vulnerable, and really scared for my family, and so to have everyone there, even if it's online, to back you up."

Today, the comments section on the *Daily Caller* article is peppered with deleted comments. Among those that remain, some include the names of Matt's wife and his employer, as well as a list of companies he's worked for as an ad copywriter. Partly as a result, Matt is both philosophical about and frustrated with the ugly side of the internet, particularly Twitter. He wonders if he's helped enable this ugliness, and also worries about Sleeping Giants being the Matt Rivitz Show. "I don't want it to be a cult of personality. We're here to do a job," he said. Collective power has always been a huge part of Sleeping Giants' identity, but Matt says there should be limits to this power. "We're not a tribe that's ready to go to war with somebody. I don't think that's healthy for the internet or society; it gives people too much power."

He tries to use his online influence to defray the tension and anger he encounters on the internet, but isn't sure it always works.

I can't say that I always do defray it; I wish I did it more.

At the end of the day, just getting attacked by racists

online, I'm over it. I always try to—when we're dealing with advertisers—keep it civil, because this thing can get really out of control really quickly.

Collectives escape their creators' intentions. Philosophically, Matt added, "People are really mean to each other online." It's the understatement of the year, coming from someone whose detractors sent death threats to his teenage kid.

Despite the newfound publicity, Matt says he's "not as present as I used to be with my family." Sleeping Giants—the urgency of it, the hungriness of it—is always on his mind. "If I don't jump on Twitter in the morning, then this thing doesn't run, so there's this responsibility, an intensity to life." He doesn't want to take money for Sleeping Giants or turn it into an official nonprofit—he says that his parents, who have nonprofit experience, have advised him against it. He fantasizes about pulling "the kill switch" sometimes, but feels like the work is more necessary than ever. But playing a leading role in Twitter's online culture war has taken an enormous psychological toll: "I think I'll look back on it and be like 'I was a clenched fist for years on end, I was always tense.'"

Nandini has also struggled, albeit differently, with claiming the power in Sleeping Giants. It's such a group effort. "I don't view any of this work as like the work of two people or the work of a handful of people. The power lies in the collective. The credit goes to the community."

After the profile ran in the *New York Times*, the photographer sent her some of the photos. She still looks at them, recognizing herself for the first time. "I look so powerful. I just never viewed myself that way." She's used to backstage roles; she once ghost-wrote for a colleague. While Matt describes himself as a "reluctant public figure," Nandini says she's eager to "become a speaker" and "take the show on the road." But how to talk about creating a movement on Twitter? It feels insubstantial, even though it isn't. "Even though we did so much work, ultimately it just goes into a bunch of posts. Like it just goes into a social media post, and what is that?"

5.

Playing the Game

Keeping the Fun in MMORPGs

About a day and a half after I started playing the video game *World of Warcraft* (WoW), a massively multiplayer online role-playing game (MMORPG), I noticed that my character, a lean "blood elf" with snappy orange leggings and a viciously effective bow and arrow attack, was suddenly dying in battle. Like millions of other people who play WoW, I'd carefully crafted my in-game character, choosing her gender, skill set, and name. Up until now—my character had reached level 8 in the game, out of a possible 120—she'd won most of her fights easily, sneaking up on and dispatching wandering lions in a relatively protected region of the WoW universe known as Eversong Woods. A warm orange-gold sunlight filtered through the tall trees of the Woods, dappling the dirt roads and rolling green hills. Every so often I'd see other players' characters floating by, their names noted above their characters' heads in purple text. We rarely interacted, except when we somehow found ourselves firing at the same enemy.

I explained my sudden death problem to Sorina, a friend I'd made while researching *WoW* guilds. Death is an inconvenience in *WoW*, rather than a permanent condition. She's been playing the game for more than a decade. She decided to come keep me company. Her character—notably fashionable, level 120—floated down out of the sky in a swirl of fabric. She considered me for a while, in my beginner hunter getup.

"I keep dying," I complained. As our characters hung out in the game, we were also connected via Discord voice chat. Often described as "Slack for gamers," Discord was created by a team of game designers in 2015 partly to let gamers connect while playing together, the exact situation Sorina and I found ourselves in.[1] Users can spin up a private Discord "server" that offers text channels and voice chat.

Sorina considered my question from her in-game vantage point. "Wait, where's your pet?" she asked.

"Where *is* my pet?" I exclaimed, noticing that the little dragon that had been tagging along behind my character for the past day and a half had somehow disappeared.

"Is your pet dead?" she asked.

"*Is my pet dead?*" I wailed, afraid that I'd lost my little dragon companion forever. Sorina patiently explained that I could use one of my keyboard buttons to summon my dragon. I pressed it, my character gave a little whistle, and my dragon materialized, healthy and ready to fight alongside me.

Fortunately for me, Sorina had appointed herself my unofficial *WoW* mentor. That won't surprise many of the people who know her; she says her role among her gamer friends is usually that of the "welcome wagon." In my case, this meant explaining every-thing from the game's complex fantasy history to how to use key-board shortcuts. Multiplayer online games—and video games in general—are famously complicated. In addition to keyboard short-cuts, learning *WoW* means learning the universe's physical spaces, the location of battles (called dungeons), and hacking the inter-face by installing user-created modifications. The makers of other MMOs—for example, the also popular *Final Fantasy XIV*—have tried to respond to that challenge by building in-game systems to encourage experienced players to share their wisdom with new-comers. In *Final Fantasy XIV*, experienced players can sign up to "mentor" newbies, and when mentors and newbies complete chal-lenges together, they both get additional rewards. *Final Fantasy XIV* also has a newcomer-only chat. *WoW* has no such formal system, relying instead on a vast network of player cooperatives—often called "guilds"—to do the job. Sorina is an admin in a guild called Terminus, which I joined as part of researching this book. In the game, she gets little out of helping me except some in-game money. In life, it's the visceral satisfaction of inducting a new person into one of her favorite activities. "I'm a very social, chit-chatty gamer. The more people I have to hang out with, the better," she said.

Media studies professor Henry Jenkins once said in a PBS essay in 2005 that "game play has always been more social than many non-gamers expect," and almost nowhere is this more evident than in MMORPGs.[2] The game designers *want* it that way: max-level battles in *WoW* are pretty much always intended to be collaborative, requiring a mix of skills; some require teams of up to twenty players.

For a long time, *WoW* was the undisputed granddaddy of modern-day MMORPGs. Blizzard Entertainment, the makers of *WoW*, no longer releases player numbers for individual games, but the company said *WoW* had more than ten million global subscribers at the end of 2014,[3] easily making it the most popular MMORPG in the world, while other estimates suggest a peak player base of twelve million.[4] Since then, unofficial estimates by fans regularly put the active *WoW* player community at several million. The next runners-up are significantly below that number.[5] The game helped define the genre, as described in this September 2019 article on the *Verge*:

> Blizzard forever changed both the RPG genre and the entire online gaming market when it launched *WoW* in 2004. It was a true modern MMORPG, and it created hundreds of millions of fans over its run. Even today, the game is still supported with new expansions, and it still has a monthly subscriber base in the millions.[6]

Sorina started playing *WoW* in 2005, when she was stationed in Nebraska with the military. One evening when she went to visit some friends, she saw they were playing *WoW* on two PCs set up next to each other. She was hooked. "I fell in love with the looks [of the game] and the social opportunities," she said. She bought a PC, signed up for internet, purchased the game, and has been playing with those friends ever since.

All Together, Now

Considering how visible they are, it's easy to think that highly experienced players make up the majority of *WoW* players. They don't, although they tend to be the most active in *WoW*'s community spaces, according to Eric St. Pierre, a guild leader who told me he also briefly worked as a game master (a customer support representative) at Blizzard.

"The raiders and the dungeon runners are the squeaky wheels that post online, so we make the news; we're the ones that everyone talks about, but we're not the majority," he said. In his time at Blizzard, Eric helped reset bugs in the game, resurrect lost characters, and even check in on reports of players who'd threatened—either in public chat or other *WoW* forums—to harm themselves. In his private gaming life, he leads Terminus, where several of those raiders and dungeon runners gather. Terminus is large, as guilds go. They have about two hundred guild members, who play more than eight hundred characters. (For ease of reference: a player is a single human individual. A "character" is an in-game avatar. It's easy—and in fact common—for a single player to have many characters, with different skill sets and professions.) Twice a week, several players get together in the evening to take on group challenges together. They'll meet up at a predetermined place in the *WoW* universe and hop into a Discord voice-chat channel. Before Discord came along, players had to organize their own private voice-chat servers in order to play together, which was time-consuming. Discord makes the process a lot easier, and has swiftly dwarfed many of its competitors in the space. It now claims fifty-six million monthly users, and is spreading outside the gaming world.[7]

But the guild's activities extend beyond the twice-weekly group raids; players can contribute in a variety of ways. Eric says he has one person who "hands out care packages when we get a new player: a backpack, a minipet to keep them company, and a couple hundred gold to get you started. That's her thing, that's what she does in the game; she farms all day and night." (In-game, of course.) He's got another player who is "one of those hilarious characters who dresses up, and she changes her outfit every single day. She's got one of the prettiest characters; her whole point is social and doing the minipet battles." Then there's a support guy: "He collects the food that our guild uses. All he does all day long is run fishing, so the rest of our group can go through and be successful. It's what he enjoys."

If this sounds like an idealized preindustrial agricultural economy, it feels a little like it to Eric, who compared group game play to an old-fashioned barn raising:

> We can get our fruit at the grocery store, it's safe for us to go out and get beef. That community-driven event of going out and harvesting is gone from American culture, and what we're doing as a guild is we're going out and reliving that cultural experience of working as a team towards a common goal. Instead of fighting the great buffalo on the range, we're fighting some kind of large water creature in the game.

Similar arguments have been made about other team sports. Before Terminus, Eric led a guild in the now-defunct *Star Wars Galaxies*, which an article in *PC Gamer* described as "an MMO with limitless potential."[8] Eric and his guild played together until the game was shut down in 2011, which he calls "one of the saddest things." When the game disappeared, Eric wondered how to maintain relationships that had become a daily part of his life. "I've known these people for years," he said of those he plays with. They'd helped each other through personal crises; he taught one guy to shave his head. He knows where they are in life: who's just built a bar in his basement, who's struggling with his medical residency. "You form those connections, and it's more than the game itself; we're forming a community as a whole." He has friends he's rarely or never met in person, but he told me he'd "trust [his] daughter with" them.

Even among gamers, Eric is atypically invested. He married a woman he met while playing WoW. They were in the same raiding group, and over six months, they started chatting about their various life's travails. They'd never met in person. Then one day, their raiding team got on voice chat together, and Eric offhandedly made a comment. His main character is female, which is not unusual—WoW is, after all, a fantasy universe—but his now-wife hadn't realized that he was, in fact, a man.

"Halfway up the ramp I get 'You're a dude!'" he said, laughing at the memory. Her consternation "caused a party wipe of forty people." By "party wipe," he means that they lost the fight. A little while later, the two of them met in person and started dating. They've been married for eleven years, and still play together.

There are as many types of guilds as there are types of players. Sorina told me about a role-playing guild she used to be in, in *The Elder Scrolls Online*, another MMORPG. All MMORPGs involve "role playing"—that's what the "RP" stands for in that lengthy acronym—but role-playing guilds are entirely driven by stories. While players in guilds like Terminus team up to beat in-game enemies, role-players use the game's characters and locations as backdrops for crafting lengthy, elaborate, and multipart ongoing tales. It can get a little *Days of Our Lives*, fantasy-style, Sorina said.

"It's all story-driven, and it's heavy community," she said. "You're building a small town of people who are role playing as shopkeepers or adventurers, and all the drama and interpersonal relationships that go with that, you create stories around that content." Her character was a captain of the town guard. She'd welcome new players by inviting them for "drinks" in the game and getting to know them. Welcoming new players is, it turns out, one of her long-standing specialties. She'd write newbies into existing stories, helping them become comfortable with eventually starting their own stories and subplots with other characters. She loved it. "I would go to the ends of *Elder Scrolls Online* and back for story," she said. But then one of the key guild leaders passed away, and the community took it "really, really hard," she said. They also wrestled with unwanted actors, what she described as "predatory" role-players, whose goal was "to manipulate, isolate, and prey upon emotionally vulnerable role players." Although they removed these players, reported them to the company that makes *The Elder Scrolls Online*, and messaged other role-playing guilds to warn them, in the end, the damage was done, and she says the community never felt the same.

Because players who play in guilds rely on those guilds so much, guild leaders have enormous, albeit collaborative, power. They set schedules, recruit members, manage supplies, and enforce rules. Guilds can fall apart over disagreements with leadership, because leaders don't care enough, or because players rebel against a particular person's leadership style. This is a lesson Sorina learned the hard way when she briefly tried to take over guild leadership of Terminus. The guild leader is the only one who can change the color of the guild's tabard (a garment that players' characters can wear in-game). She liked that part, but she soon found herself with a lot of unwanted responsibility. Guild members began coming to her with requests to make special badges, or ranks, for players in the guild. At first, these requests seemed harmless, and she complied. What she didn't realize was that a slow but angry revolution was fomenting in response to her changes:

> All I was doing was what guild members were requesting, and it never occurred to me that is exactly what happens with these other guilds. Guild leaders are just like "Sure, why not," and then before they know it it's like categorizing guildies and putting rankings and creating those divisions within the guild.

Those divisions eventually proved toxic. She gave up her leadership role, and got briefly booted from the guild for her trouble.

The expulsion lasted all of fifteen minutes, and she's now back as an admin, but she learned a valuable lesson about herself: "I think the best way to describe the way I treat gaming and the way I treat social situations [is that] I'm like a campaigner. I have to have a greater thing that I'm campaigning for, but I can't be the leader myself."

Eric, meanwhile, says he "hates authority"—but Sorina says he just hates when people use authority badly. That's why he disliked some of his prior guilds. Top *WoW* guilds—the ones that compete to be the first in the world to finish a newly released raid, for example—play the kinds of schedules that would make a pro sports team blink. Almost three years ago, the leader of world #1 *WoW* guild Method told *PCGamesN* that during a big raid, their players spent fourteen hours a day in-game, often for days at a time.[9] Most players aren't aiming for these titles, but intensity trickles down. Eric briefly played in a guild that required five to seven nights of playtime a week, for six hours at a time. He got exhausted and stressed. The game he loved stopped being fun. He left, and decided to start a guild of his own.

Terminus, which bills itself as a "family-friendly" guild, has only two rules: have fun, and don't stop other people from having fun. By and large, Eric says, he trusts his players to manage themselves and each other. In the time they've been playing together, he's only had to remove two players. One of them, a highly skilled and highly ranked player, started sending unkind messages to other players about what he perceived as their subpar gameplay. The guild leaders warned him to stop, and he didn't. Then one night, when neither Eric nor Sorina were there, they heard that the player went on a white supremacist rant—while on voice chat with the guild. He got kicked out. The other expellee was a similar case: a player who, they were told, had told other players to kill themselves. That person got the boot, too. In making these decisions, Eric points out that what happens in-game has wide-reaching consequences. In the case of the racist ranter, Eric notes that the guild includes a "rainbow" of people, of all different backgrounds. In the case of the other player, he notes that players in the guild may be struggling with mental health, and "that little push can go a long way."

But a lot of the work of guild management is more subtle negotiation. For example, he mentioned two players who differ in their opinions of how to give feedback to other players on their game performance:

> When things get intense, one guy prefers that we be very blunt and simply say "You are bad, you need to fix this, do this amount of damage," and he's not wrong; that information does need to be communicated. However, the other individual is like "No, we need to worry about their feelings, we need to build them up and make sure they understand that they're doing their best, encourage them," and he's also right. . . . These two guys probably on a weekly basis are butting heads. That's fine, they've been friends for nine years now.

In situations like this, he tries to find a "third way" that accommodates both people's preferences. He paraphrased a famous

Bruce Lee quote: "Empty your mind. Be formless, shapeless—like water. Now you put water in a cup; it becomes the cup." A good guild leader, Eric says, should be like water: adaptable to their surroundings and their players' needs. It means nurturing and respecting disagreements. He mentioned several times that people in the guild don't always agree with one another. They don't ignore politics, but it goes into a separate space. If members of the guild want to talk about a topic like gun rights, they'll make a channel for it. "If you want to talk about it, you're welcome to sit here and talk to us; if you're not interested, don't be here, we don't want to offend you," Eric said.

Because players are having fun, it's easy to overlook the enormous work required of guild leaders to keep a guild running smoothly. Leiandros "Lee" Foxworthy—the name means "lion" in Greek, he says—refers to this invisible work of running a guild as "emotional labor."[10] He started his guild—Bring the C'Thunder, the name being a pun on *WoW* lore—in July 2018. The guild's mission statement, which Lee shared with me via email, focuses on the intersection of gaming and non-gaming identity:

Will Wipe for Achievements and Bring the C'Thunder will work to achieve excellence and meaningful progress with each raid tier, while fostering a community of warm and welcoming members. Every person has value outside of the game, and every person matters. Community is an internal and external aspect of everything we do, and we have a responsibility to our members and to the world to do everything we can to make the world a little brighter.

Lee's guild is partly an effort to create spaces for players like himself. Lee is a trans man, a fact Lee is open about both in-game and out. Before Lee came out, while still playing WoW and living as a woman, there were "all kinds of really gross things said to me." Lee's raiding team told him not to talk during raids, because his voice was too distracting. When Lee came out as trans, some of those players weren't cool with it. "I was like, 'Bye, Felicia,'" Lee told me.

Lee started running raids freelance—popping into other communities and leading a raid that other players could sign up to join. Lee wanted to create an environment for folks who might not feel comfortable in "more aggressive or male-type" gaming circles, and did it by setting clear boundaries on the conversation:

> I would start my raids saying "Any -isms of any kind and I will just remove you, but we're going to have fun." A lot of LGBT or minorities or women started to wait for my raids because they knew it would be a safe place for them to be able to talk.

When news arrived that a new WoW expansion was on the horizon, a few of Lee's regular raid companions suggested that he start a guild, which became Bring the C'Thunder. The guild's values include "radical kindness," "inclusivity," and "community." Since then, Lee says it's expanded and grown, finding appreciation and acceptance among other players.

"It's nice to see people so open and receptive to our culture and our policies," Lee said. Opting into the guild means opting into Lee's values. In the mission statement, Lee describes himself as the guild's "benevolent dictator" and says, "If you find your-self in harsh disagreement with these policies, please just show yourself the door." Lee has a circle of officers who help with ad-ministration and give advice. It includes an ombudsman whose job is to listen to and process member complaints. And in a gam-ing landscape that is often dominated by men, the C'Thunder leadership is majority female, Lee said.

While Eric talked about being "like water," Lee talked about love languages. "I just need to know the love language of all of my raiders to be able to know how to talk to them . . . and that's emotional labor that I enjoy," Lee said. For example, some play-ers respond well to words of affirmation—once Lee figures that out, he knows that praise is the way to get them to do even bet-ter in battle. Lee also learns the ins and outs of their schedules. Whenever he's interacting with his guildies, Lee's "making men-tal notes, like 'this person has two dogs they love' or 'this person lives in another country so I know their schedule is crazy' or 'this person always feels insecure about being involved despite hav-ing been with us for a year and a half.'" Lee is inexhaustible in unearthing and absorbing these details, in part because the guild's philosophy extends beyond the game: "If people have lost jobs or had children, we want to make sure we support them as people, and not just a set of pixels that performs a role for us in a raid." This philosophy sets the guild apart—and it also means Lee and his husband have given money to fellow players who were having trouble making ends meet. Once, they paid for a year's worth of formula for a fellow player who'd recently had a baby.

ANIKA GUPTA

Every team includes some highly skilled players, and others who are improving. Like Eric, Lee struggles with how to give feedback to guild members on how to improve. In some guilds, feedback happens publicly—players will comment to each other in a chat that everyone can see or hear. But C'Thunder's members include a lot of people who "have experienced trauma," Lee said, and they don't want to "publicly embarrass them." So they have a feedback format: the person giving feedback will usually reach out via private message and start with a question about a recent battle, like "Hey, did you know that this happened?" After that, the critique might go something like "I noticed this ability didn't get interrupted; from my experience, it's easier to use this add-on that tells you when to interrupt." Lee told me that presenting feedback as a suggestion or wrapping it in a personal anecdote is more compassionate, even though it takes more tact and more effort.

Another source of conflict: team size is capped by the game, and every so often, the guild has to go through the process of selecting players. They invariably have more applicants than spots, which might leave some of the rejected players with uncomfortable memories of being picked last in gym class. Freely admitting that it's been a struggle to manage this process, Lee says they've learned here, too—before publishing a list of players who've been selected, they'll send a private message to everyone who applied to let them know the results. Professional recruiters sometimes do the same, but Lee's guild is informal, run by volunteers.

Partly owing to his background, Lee thinks a lot about how these teams, and the broader game community, can create positive impact. "I firmly believe that if you are in a position where you are able to access something that other people can't, that's a form of privilege," Lee said. By Lee's logic, being a good raid team is a "privilege." Beating the hardest challenges in the game will often come with exclusive prizes: a fancy piece of weaponry, or a fun mount (a creature that carries players place to place; a little like a new car, if a new car had ears, wings, or the ability to fly). Players who aren't experienced enough—or don't have enough friends—to field a team will never be able to get these exclusive rewards. So sometimes, members join in for "charity streaming" and "charity carries." The guild will partner with other communities to broadcast themselves on Twitch while playing challenging content, and they'll hold lotteries for players to get carried through the content. Teams like Lee's will "carry" these players—basically, they'll bring them into the fight, drop them off somewhere, kill all the monsters, and share the prizes. Although they cannot put a set price on charity carries, they'll add a link to a donation page. Lee says they've raised thousands of dollars for charities like St. Jude Children's Research Hospital and the Leukemia & Lymphoma Society, and are planning on more. The community that they partner with for charity carries includes some of the top players in the world, so longtime players can also get a kick out of raiding with people they admire.

Lee seems to enjoy running the guild, but there are times when he acknowledges that "compassion fatigue" sets in. He knows all the guild's two hundred players by voice, and "that's a lot of people to know at least one fact about." At times like this, which Lee describes as "emotionally exhausted," he'll turn to his guild officers and ask for help. "You cannot do it by yourself," Lee said.

Earlier on, Lee referred to guild management as emotional labor. Other moderators have used a similar term in conversations with me. Arlie Hochschild, the sociologist who coined the term in the early 1980s, recently defined it in an interview with the *Atlantic* writer Julie Beck:

> . . . the work, for which you're paid, which centrally involves trying to feel the right feeling for the job. This involves evoking and suppressing feelings. Some jobs require a lot of it, some a little of it . . . while you may also be doing physical labor and mental labor, you are crucially being hired and monitored for your capacity to manage and produce a feeling.[11]

Guild leaders are not paid, although rewards can come in intangible forms: greater recognition within the community, status within a guild. As volunteers, their "hiring" can happen in a variety of ways—sometimes they take on the role when a guild forms; other times they're more formally recruited by other guild leaders. Many leaders are extensively monitored by their communities, and as Sorina's case demonstrates, they can be recalled. The mechanisms for recall are often informal—an accumulation of complaints sent to another admin via DM, for example, rather than an outright election—but communities are clear about making their frustrations felt. And when leaders do change roles, this can change their perception of their own identity, and not just in the game. And even though there's no financial recompense for their efforts, guild leaders spend a lot of time managing other people's feelings. Lee gave me an example:

> We have a member who has pretty awful depression. [They're] convinced [they're] terrible, even though [they've] been with us through a few trimmings of the guild team. The effort it takes to reassure [them] that yes, we would like [them] around and no, [they aren't] terrible is pretty substantial. There are three of us who put effort into that. And then we need to deal with how that affects the morale of everyone else on the team. Similarly, one of my officers needs periodic positive reinforcement and reassurance that they are indeed the best person for the job.

In Beck's article, she cites another writer, Gemma Hartley, who defines emotional labor more broadly:

> It is the unpaid, invisible work we do to keep those around us comfortable and happy. It envelops many other terms associated with the type of care-based labor I described in my article: emotion work, the mental load, mental burden, domestic management, clerical labor, invisible labor.

Not every guild leader thinks about emotional management to the extent that Lee does, but both Lee and Eric described emotional balancing acts, and the work involved in making sure players felt heard and satisfied. Lee also does a lot of "care-based labor"—thinking about and getting to know individual guild members. Lee also does a lot of clerical work, which often takes the form of farming or tracking down the in-game supplies— things like potions—that teams need for raids. If the idea of emotional labor resonates with moderators, it may be because so much of the work of maintaining a community is deeply invisible, and powered by care.

Although *WoW* is famous for its unique and complex guild structure, I heard similar themes in conversations with people who led guilds in other games. Icarus Twine, who told me he played his first *Final Fantasy* game when he was six years old, started running his *Final Fantasy XIV* guild—in *Final Fantasy*, the preferred term is "free company"—when the previous leader went, as he put it, "AWOL."[12] His free company has thirty-eight members and organizes events twice a week. He often thinks about how to make newer players feel welcome, rather than intimidated. Their free company has a Discord bot that members can use to tag themselves into an upcoming event "so people don't feel [threatened] when they want to join an event but don't want to ask." They also include players of all skill levels, partly for reasons of morale: "It's important for us to have varying degrees of skill so not only can they request help, it doesn't give the feeling to new players of 'I'm so new and unskilled at this game, these guys are way too endgame to want to help me.'" The emotional work of managing a group may be harder for large guilds and guilds that accept strangers, because these guilds are constantly wrestling with newcomers. But these challenges exist even for smaller, friends-

and-family guilds. Angelus Demonus[13] participates in a free company with a small group of friends who play *Final Fantasy XIV* together. They've been playing together for years, ever since *Final Fantasy XI* was launched. When they went dormant in *Final Fantasy XI*, they created a Facebook group to stay in touch. Because they'd stayed in touch, it made natural sense to team up again for *Final Fantasy XIV*, the next game in the series. Angelus says that, until 2018, he'd never met any of his game friends in person—not that it mattered. "I have a friend I've known for almost thirteen or fourteen years, and I met them for the first time last year," he said. Unlike the guilds I examined earlier, which formed partly so players could find raiding partners, Angelus's group is primarily social. He's not really into team challenges—he prefers to play solo—and he's seen what happened with raiding teams: it "almost felt like an obligation to be in them. You had to be in that thing full-time, you had to commit to all these events." Instead, he formed a more casual group, where people could "chill, talk, play whatever you want." Anyone can join, but "we're connected by the fact that we like each other's company." In order to keep it civil, he says he has simple rules, which include no talk about politics or religion. There are about twenty to thirty players, and while they were initially open to strangers, they now accept only friends-of-friends. The only troublesome person he can think of is one player who kept showing up drunk and saying inappropriate things in the chat—a little like that one troublesome friend everyone has offline.

MMOs are famous time sucks, and I quickly started spending hours in *WoW*. I hit level 40, then kept climbing. At one point, I played my first dungeon, which involved signing up for the game's random matching system and being put into a short-term group with several strangers, specifically for the duration of that fight. (Although people will often play more complex dungeons with their guildies, I was running a quick and low-level dungeon, for which the matching system would suffice.) I was worried about how this matching would turn out—I'd read messages on newcomer WoW forums about toxic players who spewed invective or criticized new players in dungeon teams. Groups can "vote" to remove a toxic player from their short-term team, but the other players in the group have to agree to the vote. With some trepidation, I submitted my character's name to the matching system. A few minutes later, I got put into a group. The game transported us to the battle: a series of dark caves and tunnels. The dungeon itself was terrifying. Unlike the quest enemies I'd fought thus far, the enemies in the dungeon refused to stand still. I shot in the wrong direction, ran off a bridge into a lake, and died twice; once, one of the other players in my party brought me back to life. "First dungeon!" I posted in the comments. As if they couldn't tell. Despite my worst fears, the other players were kind. When I died, they retrieved me. "No worries!" one of them said. After it was all over and I'd gathered up the money and goods I'd won, I checked WoW's chat. "Reputation with Guild increased by 125," it told me. I had no idea what that meant, or if it was even in response to the dungeon, but it felt pretty good to think that the other people in my guild, wherever they were at that moment, thought better of me.

6.

For All the World to See

Moderating Reddit

No matter how hard a creator tries, it's impossible for them to fully control how people interact with the technology they build. Once users enter a universe, they turn it to their own purposes. Reseph, a longtime online community builder and moderator, learned this lesson in his teens.[1] In 2003, bored with merely playing games online, he decided to build his own. His MUD, an early version of a multiplayer online game, drew on Japanese feudal mythology and lore. Players could create and join clans, contribute to forums, and battle one another and enemies. When he designed the game, he scattered pieces of superpowered gemstones throughout the world. When players stumbled upon a gemstone shard, they'd immediately enter PVP mode, an intense game mode where they would fight other players. There was no way to turn PVP mode off. Over time, though, players began to subvert Reseph's design. Instead of using the gemstone shards to battle, they started using them as currency.

"Here you are in the same room as someone else and you're open to being attacked, but instead you're trading," Reseph said to me, still sounding surprised about it. Since then, he's seen similarly unexpected outcomes in other forums. Reseph has had a long online life, during which he's been a creator, moderator, and participant in online communities. He says he "grew up" on traditional message boards, where he "formed lifelong relationships" with other community members. They talked about why they loved the game, and sometimes teamed up to play together.

He found Reddit a little more than a decade ago. Reddit is, by their own estimate, one of the most popular sites on the internet. It contains more than 130,000 active communities, each managed by volunteer moderators. When Reseph discovered the site, he told me, it "wasn't too huge," and there "definitely was a community." He and other gamers would talk about upcoming games and gaming industry news. Compared to the other private communities he'd joined, Reddit felt less personal: "You're in these public spaces, people are coming and going, so it's hard to grasp who's who sometimes." In October 2008, partly as an experiment, he decided to create a subreddit for the video game *Final Fantasy XI*. The game had been out for several years and already had established online fan communities, but he thought "Why not?" The subreddit grew slowly. He says the subreddit's culture was influenced in part by the culture of the game: *Final Fantasy XI* was what he describes as a "hard-core" MMO. When characters died in the game, they were docked a game level. It took anywhere from ten to thirty hours to level up, which meant death was more than an inconvenience—so players put a lot of energy into not dying, and because battles were often collabora-tive, "you had to rely on everybody else." This led to what he de-scribed as an intensely collaborative culture among players. But then the game developers changed the structure, making death less costly (and possibly making the game more accessible for casual players). Reseph says a lot of hard-core fan sites shut down in the wake of the change, possibly due to the restructur-ing or to other factors. The *Final Fantasy XI* subreddit picked up some of the slack, but remained small; today he describes the subreddit's culture as more "casual." It still has daily discussions, but those discussions are partly driven by nostalgia.

Among those who study online communities, Reddit is inter-esting because of its size, as well as the way its community and structure have evolved as the site has grown. There's no one Red-dit experience. The site contains thousands of discussion forums, called subreddits, each managed by its own volunteer modera-tors. According to their own official estimates, Reddit is the fifth-most visited website in the United States, with 330 million monthly users, and 21 billion monthly pageviews.[2] That visitor number puts Reddit on par with Wikipedia's 22 billion monthly pageviews.[3] Individual subreddits have achieved lives of their own—the Ask Me Anything subreddit has hosted reader Q&As with Bill Gates, Barack Obama, and Madonna, among other luminaries.

Community moderators, in uneasy balance with Reddit's paid administrators, exert a large influence over the site's overall culture, and will often share information with one another. Vet-eran technology journalist Adrian Chen describes moderator cul-ture on Reddit:

Today Reddit is governed, insofar as it's governed at all, by a cabal of high-powered moderators who coordinate with administrators in private forums. The most influential of these forums, Modtalk, allows access only to moderators who oversee subreddits with a combined subscriber base of at least 25,000. A convoluted moderator culture has developed, full of intrigue and drama.[4]

The site is well-known for its controversies, many of which have turned on the question of how much Reddit's paid administrators should try to control their community's behavior. In 2012, Chen published an article that revealed the real identity of Violentacrez, a volunteer moderator who infamously ran a huge subreddit devoted to sexually charged images of minors.[5] The company's official leadership had faced enormous public criticism for allowing subreddits like Violentacrez's (they did eventually pass stricter rules about sexual content).

In 2015, several volunteer moderators exercised their power by shutting down moderator activity on their subreddits, a strike that eventually became known as the Reddit Blackout. The blackout began when Reddit fired an employee whose job was to be a liaison to the community, but it quickly grew to envelop other issues, like how Reddit leadership involved the community in site-wide decision-making. It doesn't help that, while Reddit generates revenue, it doesn't pay a cent to any of the volunteer moderators who spend hours—sometimes well beyond a part-time job's commitment—making the subreddits run.

Not long after Reseph started his *Final Fantasy XI* subreddit, the game developers announced that a new game was on the horizon: *Final Fantasy XIV*, the next iteration in the series.

This time, Reseph was ahead of the curve; in 2010, he started a subreddit for *Final Fantasy XIV*. This subreddit has grown into Reseph's largest venture yet. At 310,000 members, this subreddit (per Reddit convention, I'll use the URL abbreviation, r/ffxiv, to refer to it) is a healthy midsize-to-large community, although Reseph doesn't put much store by the official subscriber count. The discussions—dozens a day—veer between gamers giving each other advice, sharing their Final Fantasy fanart, and giving the moderators feedback on how the forum runs. This last category of conversation can get extremely intense; the subreddit is very active. Reseph says they get between eight hundred thousand and one million pageviews on any given day, and back in July 2019—at their peak—they hit eighty million pageviews in one month. Eighty million is comparable to the website of a major national publication, and this is just one subreddit, staffed and managed entirely by eighteen volunteers.

Moderating subreddits, Reseph says, requires a keen understanding of how "cultures change." That change has been evident in his own subreddit. *Final Fantasy XIV*, the game, has had two iterations. The first came out in 2010 and proved unpopular. In those early days, the subreddit was "a small and tight-knit community." Reseph says his three-to-four-person moderation team didn't really do a lot of day-to-day moderation. The discussions, he said, were "higher quality," which seems to mean they featured substantive discussions about the game. The moderators didn't allow a lot of image-based posts. Then the Final Fantasy developers took the unusual step of completely redoing and reissuing the game in 2013. As the game's relaunch neared, Reseph began to realize that the community was growing and changing, and the moderation team would also have to grow and adapt. "We had graphs of traffic charts, we kind of knew we were growing, [but] that isn't the core thing," he said. "The core thing is if we're seeing a lot more rule violations occurring." The increasing number of rules violations, he said, told him "We were entering an Eternal September."

Eternal September is a popular term in message board and online community lore. It refers to the moment in time when a site's existing userbase and culture are overwhelmed by new users who don't know the site's rules. The original example is now canonical: until September 1993, Usenet, an ancestor to many modern forums and online communities, had a small and dedicated userbase with established norms. Then, that September, America Online (remember AOL?) started offering Usenet access to millions of users. New users, unfamiliar with existing conventions, overwhelmed forums and shifted their culture, often irretrievably.

Although all members of an online community can violate rules, newcomers are more likely to err. In 2019, the researcher J. Nathan Matias published the results of an experiment he conducted in partnership with the moderators of r/science, a thirteen-million-member subreddit devoted to discussing research and scientific results. In the preface to his paper about the experiment, he describes how challenging newcomer posts are for the moderators:

In July 2016, moderators removed 494 newcomer comments per day, 39.1% of all of the comments they removed on average and 52.3% of all newcomer comments. First-time commenters were also more likely to violate community policies than more experienced commenters. These newcomers may not yet be aware of community policies against abusive language, insulting jokes, or personal medical anecdotes.[6]

The rule against abusive language might be widespread (although how people define abusive language can vary), but the rule against personal medical anecdotes is specific to r/science.

Reseph's r/ffxiv has some rules that are common across many subreddits. Their first rule is "Be civil and respectful; no name shaming." But some of the rules are specific to video game forums and to r/ffxiv in particular—for example, rule 6a, which deals with fanart: "When posting content including commissioned, drawn, or discovered fanworks, the author/artist must be credited with their name(s) included in the title."

Reseph also noticed that the number of concurrent users on the subreddit had begun to climb—another thing that makes life more challenging for moderators. "Once we hit seven hundred to one thousand concurrent users, we're moving toward Eternal September, which just means toxic comments go from ten to one hundred a week," he said. "You need to make sure you've planned for that before it happens." They needed more clearly defined rules and better tools in the back end for managing the moderation queue (the list of posts and messages awaiting moderators' attention). For example, they started using an automated tool to append explanations for why they removed a particular comment.

Managing a larger subreddit involves liaising differently with the subreddit's community. As the forum has grown, it's become a more public and contested space. This publicity is less about access—r/ffxiv is visible to anyone who comes to the URL—than about the scale of discussion and who gets input into the community rules. In the early days, when he started both of his subreddits, Reseph said he created rules based on "what kind of culture [I wanted] to instill in the community." Now, he says, it's a lot more about the community: "What do they want to see, what don't they want to see?"

Establishing consensus among thousands of community members can be an impossible task. In response to demand, the moderator team has tried to increase what Reseph referred to as "transparency"—the extent to which moderator decisions are public and open for community comment. The change is evident in their moderator hiring process. In the early days of r/ffxiv (and still for r/ffxi) the moderator hiring process was simple: if the moderating team felt like they needed a new moderator, they'd put out a call for submissions and then decide who fit their needs.

Today, the moderator hiring process for r/ffxiv is more public-facing, and involves several stages of vetting. Every year or so Reseph will check in with the existing moderators to see if they need to hire anyone. If they do, they'll open up applications by posting on the subreddit. When people apply for a moderator spot, their application will get posted to a separate public Reddit forum, where community members can comment and vote. The existing moderator team takes these votes into account when choosing a pool of finalists. Then they conduct interviews, a process that can take weeks. After that, they usually choose two to three new moderators to join their team.

As the forum has grown, it's become more crucial to involve the existing community in decision-making. In part, the pressure to be transparent comes from the community itself, which is vocal about things it doesn't like, and which can easily abandon r/ffxiv for other forums if it doesn't care for the moderation style. But there's also the fact that the forum is a visible part of the *Final Fantasy* ecosystem. Square Enix, the company that makes the game, doesn't acknowledge the subreddit in an official capacity, but Reseph says the developers are "aware" of the forum.

"As a moderator, you're in a public space, you're being scrutinized," Reseph said. He said that r/ffxiv moderators get recognized in the game, in related Discord servers, and on Twitter.

There are several ways for the community to offer feedback to the moderators, and when Reseph and I spoke, he was in the process of introducing one more: a monthly feedback thread. This feedback thread would be in addition to a "meta" forum where members can share feedback on the moderation style; ModMail, which is Reddit's direct messaging system; and a feedback form. Reseph and I spoke over the Thanksgiving holiday weekend; that Sunday, the r/ffxiv moderation team launched the new feature. Two days later, it had nearly one hundred comments. Many of the comments are several paragraphs long, with links.

Reading these comments illustrates not just people's desire to contribute but also the moderators' challenge when it comes to crafting a consensus. In one feedback conversation, a user questions why there are so many "downvotes" (a post that gets repeatedly downvoted on Reddit moves farther and farther down the page) on r/ffxiv posts. In response, Reseph linked to a post he made years ago, gently reminding people that the solution lay in their hands:

> Sometimes we get threads here where people are concerned with the downvotes in the subreddit. Downvotes aren't uncommon, especially in larger subreddits like ours. The problem isn't so much downvotes, but a lack of upvotes.
>
> Don't be picky with upvotes. Did you like a post? Was it interesting or funny? Informative? Throw some upvotes their way! Sometimes we get repeat posts like questions; but if you think they did some research and maybe the discussion brought something new to the table, throw it an upvote!

But this comment spawned its own spin-off discussion: How should people use and interpret the upvote? Does it indicate agreement, or merely appreciation?

In their responses on the monthly feedback thread, the moderators ask for additional information, clarify policy, and provide charts of behavior on the forum. (In response to the downvote question, Reseph calculated roughly how much downvoting occurred in r/ffxiv versus other game-specific subreddits.) A few days after rolling out the monthly feedback thread, he told me they planned to have a moderation team meeting to discuss the results and possibly change the rules.

There are times, he told me, when it's impossible to make everyone happy. In the early days of the forum, the rules forbade image-based posts. As the community grew, some fans wanted to post their fanart. The moderators changed the rules to permit fanart, but the change sparked—and continues to fuel—displeasure among members who believe the forum should be reserved for discussion of the game. Longtime member Icarus Twine told me via Discord chat that "Sometimes it's hard to see the line between 'art posts' and 'low-effort art.'" At the same time, he said he appreciates the effort the moderators put in, which he's become more aware of the longer he's been in the community.

"When I first started, [r/ffxiv] was quite nice, lots of decent people with hardly any opposing opinions, but now [that] I'm more on the 'inside' of Reddit I see that that's more so because the moderators do a lot to keep the peace," he said. He's part of several subreddits, but r/ffxiv is the only one he ever posts in. He appreciates "the amount of reports, false reports, bans, etc. [the moderators] have to deal with on a daily basis," he said, as well as the fact that moderators "calm down situations I usually avoid." He attributed some of the positivity of r/ffxiv to the game's underlying community: "r/ffxiv stands out the most compared to a lot of other communities because everyone here/there has a genuine love and respect for the game the subreddit is based on." He said he tries to help out the moderators: "If something needs bringing to mods' attention, I'll send it their way." While his own involvement in the forum has dropped off slightly, he said he still visits r/ffxiv every day.

Even though external cultures influence the subreddit's culture, negotiating among the many users of a public, popular Reddit forum is an enormous and ongoing task. As the subreddit's profile has grown, Reseph continually wonders how much transparency the community needs, and how much puts the moderators at risk. For example, although Reddit provides logs of individual moderator behavior, the moderator team doesn't make those logs available for community comment, partly to protect moderators from harassment. Like the community itself, moderator harassment often spills over into other forums. A couple of r/ffxiv moderators started getting harassed in a Discord channel for *Final Fantasy XIV* team recruiting. The harassment came from a particular section of the *Final Fantasy XIV* community, says Reseph. Eventually, a couple of those moderators stepped down from the moderation team out of frustration.

From Text to Voice and Back Again: The Challenges of Discord

Moderating a popular online community—especially for video gamers, who spend a lot of time online—also means adapting to new technologies, like Discord, a service that allows users to build closed social networks for their communities. The r/ffxiv moderator team runs a dedicated Discord for their community. They joined Discord years ago, when the tool was still new, and became an official partner server, which means "we represent Discord and have more rules." The r/ffxiv Discord has nearly three dozen text channels, where members share game updates, plan meetups, ask for help, and—in one channel, anyway—post photos of food. Part of the moderators' motivation for getting on Discord was to be present on a service that gamers increasingly used to connect with one another.

But Discord, designed to make it easier for groups to play together, isn't necessarily designed for large, more public communities. Reseph, who *also* moderates a tiny Discord for his friends in *Final Fantasy XIV*, described the difference:

> Free companies don't need moderation tools that much. If somebody says something offensive in our fc, we can delete it.[7] You're private and can boot somebody, and you don't get public scrutiny. They have a lot less need for those tools.

The r/ffxiv community is used to r/ffxiv moderation. Discord doesn't always offer these types of moderation tools natively, he said:

> In native Discord, someone violates a rule, you remove that comment and maybe warn the user. What happens if a day later the user comes back and says, "I never made a rule violation"? You don't have that anymore; you've deleted it. Discord has no logging.

Instead, moderators have built their own Discord tools that mimic the services they have on Reddit: things like post tagging or removal explanation. Reseph belongs to a Discord server for moderators who've expanded their subreddits to include Discord, where they trade advice and links.

The advent of Discord has also introduced a new challenge into the moderators' universe: voice chat. Reseph described their experiences trying to respond to a report that a user was violating rules in voice chat:

> Someone will complain to mods that a user is harassing someone in voice chat. You enter voice chat and nobody's talking; what do you do? . . . One of our mods sat in voice chat for two hours and there was no activity. . . . Especially [for] those of us at work, you can't sit in a voice-chat channel all day.

Without a recording, he said, "there's no way to validate" what individual users might or might not have said in voice chat. Earlier in 2019, a team of researchers interviewed twenty-five moderators with experience moderating Discord voice channels, and found that the biggest challenge moderators faced was that voice chat is effectively "ephemeral"—wrongdoing leaves no record.[8] Violations included harassing other users in chat, disrupting voice conversations with other loud noises, and screaming in a channel. Moderators in the study responded to the challenge in a variety of ways. One moderator asked another user to secretly record harassing behavior. While this method created a record, the researchers pointed out that nonconsensual recording isn't always legal.[9] In a *Medium* post about the study, one of its authors, Aaron Jiang, suggested one possible solution: "Designers can implement systems that detect volumes that may be uncomfortable for humans, and temporarily mute these loud accounts."[10]

That's essentially the approach taken by Eric St. Pierre, who leads a guild in *World of Warcraft* and is also a volunteer moderator for a gaming server on Ventrilo, a voice-chat service and one of the predecessors to Discord. Although the Ventrilo server is down from its peak usership—mainly because Discord has grown more popular as an alternative—he said that the effort of moderating Ventrilo has gone down dramatically ever since one of the moderators built a bot to help manage voice moderation. The bot detects when voice levels in a Ventrilo chat have risen above comfortable levels, and texts the moderators. It'll also automatically remove an account if two-thirds of the people in the channel report that account as causing trouble. It "does take away a bit of the personal touch," said Eric, and there's always a chance that users might gang up on one another and require human intervention While tools like the audio auto-moderator can help moderators, it cannot supplant them. That's especially true the larger or more active a community becomes. Reseph's experience demonstrates that as communities expand in member activity, they expand in moderator complexity: the types of decisions moderators make, and the forces holding moderators accountable, increase.

Reseph has been moderating, in one way or another, for nearly twenty years. He's seen the internet change and grow, and has shaped some of these changes himself. He's never made a penny from it, and he said he's never wanted to stop. Moderating r/ffxiv has expanded his knowledge of the game, he said, especially in-game activities, like crafting, that he doesn't person-ally participate in. He's learned things about the game's universe that he would otherwise never have known. Despite its scale, an MMORPG can sometimes feel like a small world: without a forum like r/ffxiv, "you would have very little insight outside of your own circle," he said.

Also, the skills he's learned as a moderator are widely appli-cable even outside of Reddit, he said:

> The day-to-day stuff is very menial; I don't know how much of that would flow over to other areas, but the big-ger picture of managing community, reading the room, and writing public posts to a community of 300K and how you're going to word that, definitely plays into pretty much anything you're doing in life.

When he's not moderating Reddit or Discord, Reseph works in information security, where his job often involves crafting mes-sages that reach thousands of internal company users.

"My experience on Reddit and moderating, that kind of flows into . . . how I'm going to write something," he said. He keeps these messages informative and brief. Another lesson he's learned from his years managing communities on the internet, which he of-fered up with the world-weariness of someone far older than his thirtysomething years: "As the internet grows older and older, people are willing to read less and less."

7.

Building a Creative Community

The Artists of YouTube

Nick Nocturne[1] wanted to become a fiction writer. He graduated from high school in 2012. A meticulous researcher, he spent three months creating what he describes as a "master binder of facts and advice and lessons in how to be a fiction writer." The compendium included articles by writers, publishers, and editors; advice on how to craft smooth sentences and develop engaging narratives. But it seemed impossible to get a book contract "if you didn't have your name already out there for something." So he decided to skip traditional publishing entirely and start creating and uploading video stories to YouTube.

He became a YouTube essayist, and today his channel, Night Mind, has a little more than four hundred thousand subscribers. For his first project, he delved into the internet's collective subconscious. He created an hour-long video that explains in detail the ins and outs of a niche but well-known web horror series called *Marble Hornets*. The *Marble Hornets* story unfolds in real time, and the characters don't necessarily let on that they're actors. The series falls into the "alternate reality game" genre, in which storytellers unspool complex narratives across multiple platforms, often interactively. Nick had been interested in ARGs for several years, and *Marble Hornets*' immersive, multi-platform storytelling quickly drew him in. "The action was happening beat for beat in your daily life; you could receive a tweet as you were going about your own life, and that was extremely exciting," he said. "No one on YouTube had really done [that] in serialized horror. I felt it was an injustice that *Marble Hornets* wasn't being talked about, because it was a massive achievement by regular guys."

Launched in 2009, *Marble Hornets*' plot centers on a group of student filmmakers. One of the filmmakers goes back to review the footage after the project has ended. He quickly realizes that there's something off about it. As he starts behaving more and more erratically, the viewer realizes that the filmmaker is being stalked by a slim, faceless man, who appears in many of the shots. *Marble Hornets* unfolds like a puzzle: the viewer has to fit the narrative together by cracking clues that appear in videos and on Twitter. At the end of the first season, it's unclear if any of the main characters are alive or dead.

Nick's *Marble Hornets* video brings together elements of a film review and a game playthrough: in an hour of brisk, mellifluously voiced-over dialogue, he recaps the entire first season, with screenshots of puzzles and plot reveals that appeared on YouTube and Twitter. He explains the various codes, draws conclusions about what happened to the characters, and offers a hypothesis of his own (with warnings for spoilers, of course) about what's going on and what might happen next.

He spent hours researching the story, writing the script, and editing the video, and the process helped him realize what he wanted to do next himself. "It was such an exhausting task, and at the same time I loved every second of it," he said. "It brought me to life."

Actually, the video brought Nick Nocturne to life. He'd stepped into a genre known as creepypasta, a funky name for something that's existed for ages: the apocryphal horror story, told around the campfire by an unreliable narrator to a terrified audience who can't quite distinguish what's fact and what's fiction. Campfire ghost stories are scary because said ghosts might slide out of the nearby forest at any moment; many creepypasta narrators strive for the same combination of mystery and uncertainty.

Nick begins his videos by inviting viewers to open their "night mind" (hence the channel's name)—to step into a darkly wooded, spooky universe where legends linger. He describes creepypasta as "a digital form of horror folk legends." The term was born in online forums as a riff on "copypasta," which refers to something that's been copied and pasted over and over again. A creepypasta is the same concept, but scarier. Creepypasta narrators—what Nick was becoming—try to play it "as straight as possible." From the beginning, he kept his legal name to himself, opting instead to become the glib, mysterious, slightly mischievous Nick Nocturne.

"This is a terrain of mystery and people with masks, fake names, so I immediately knew that Nick Nocturne was a way to deliver the content," Nick said. He created Twitter and Tumblr accounts for Night Mind and Nick Nocturne. The Twitter bio reads like a pastiche of horror tropes past and present. At one point, it read: "Shapeshifting demon in the form of a 4-eyed humanoid black cat monster playing a male YouTube Elvira for modern art." He offers even more zany details on Tumblr: "Queen Mother's most ill-behaved son wasting eternity telling campfire stories to human prey on the internet." Elvira is a black-gowned horror show hostess from the 1980s, while the Queen Mother is the mythological demon Lilith, a popular figure in horror lore.

Nick's first video is an eerie essay, complete with smoky visual effects that swirl in the video's background. He breaks *Marble Hornets*' spooky, absorbing, and fragmented tale into understandable components. The most popular videos on YouTube at the time were shorter vlogs or tutorials. But he was helped by a change he could never have predicted. YouTube, he says, changed its recommendation algorithm to favor longer videos with consistent watch times, rather than short entries with large but uncommitted audiences.

By the time Nick uploaded the video in 2015, *Marble Hornets* was already over, but its mysteries continued to absorb its legions of fans, and many of them found his video. Four years after Nick first uploaded it, "Marble Hornets: Explained—Season One" has nearly a million views and almost 3,500 comments. "Damn it, Night Mind. I come here to have the mysteries of horror picked apart for me so I can free myself from the fear. It's no good if you scare me too," wrote one unnerved viewer several years ago. Others appreciated Nick's style, including what would become his trademark smooth voice: "Love the voice and the ambiance, and have the utmost respect for the amount of work put into the videos. <3 " wrote one. "I've watched this series of yours so much I put on the playlist as background noise for bed 😄 ," wrote another. The critical comments note that the sound editing could use work.

"Overwhelmed with joy," Nick jumped into the comments and tried to respond to everyone, trading notes with people who were interested in the puzzles and responding to the comments about his editing.

At first it was easy to respond to all his commenters, because there weren't many of them. Being in the comments felt like a conversation among fans. "It was so much fun to go down there [to the comments section]," he said. He also started working on explainer videos for seasons two and three of *Marble Hornets*. He posted the season two explainer six days after the first video went up.

"I am a huge *Marble Hornets* fan and in watching this I can't believe that there were so many things I missed," wrote one fan four years ago, on the video explainer for season two. "It's an awesome feeling to make these discoveries, isn't it?" Nick replied in the comments. Another commenter pointed out a detail that Nick seemed to have missed in his video recap, and he replied by mentioning that he *did* notice it, but wanted to save it for another video: "It almost HURT me not to say anything about the lighter when it showed up, but I knew for the sake of story and surprise, I had to keep quiet." These exchanges are interwoven with more recent comments, from people who've come to the video in 2016 or later. Nick is notably absent from most of these recent conversations. As his videos gained popularity, he says the YouTube comments changed as well, and he stopped spending as much time there.

"Over time you see a lot of jokers, a lot more negativity. The crowd that you gelled with, that you wanted to attract, [becomes] a little bit harder to see," he said. Part of this is the way YouTube works: comments aren't filterable, and posts by frequent or loyal commenters don't appear at the top. As a result, gaining more viewers comes with a "tradeoff . . . you're going to end up reaching a lot of people who are not the audience that you intended."

Part of it is due to the fact that Nick's career coincided with a time when "YouTube creator" was going from "hobby" to full-time profession, supported by a host of platforms and tools that closed the gap between creators and listeners. In addition to YouTube and its (challenging to moderate) comments section, Nick started to explore Tumblr, Twitter, Patreon, and Discord as places to organize exclusive chats and conversations with fans.

Tumblr, driven by images, became a place for fanart. Fans regularly send him their drawings of his four-eyed cat persona, which he reblogged (reposted) as often as he could, moved, he said, by the "effort they put in." There's a fan-created drawing of the four-eyed cat in an elaborate purple vest. The fan who sent it in apologized for the "low quality" of the image; Nick reposted it with the reply, "Both the photo and the art are just fine. Good work, thank you! A wonderful bit of Halloween attire." On another fan image, of the black cat giving an alarmingly toothy, predatory smile, Nick commented, "This is the face I make when it's time to get rid of curious interlopers."

Nick loves playing around with his host's personality. When we talked, Nick compared Nick Nocturne to a "WWE wrestler"—a character rather than "a real person." The character has shifted over time and is different on different platforms. On YouTube, he's somewhat distant. On Tumblr and Twitter, he gets a bit more personable. In one post, a fan asked if "not safe for work" images of his persona were okay; he replied, "Art of any kind is an honor, and NM as a channel is far from being for people under 18 anyway."

The material on the main Night Mind YouTube channel skews "dark"—creepy, ghostly, occasionally filled with blood. Adult material can do well on YouTube, but the platform's algorithms, according to Nick, favor more family-friendly material, which has made it harder for him to build an audience, as well as an income stream. Like many YouTube artists, he makes money from YouTube advertisements, but this income can be irregular and unsustainable. His *Marble Hornets* videos were well received, but when he tried to upload videos about more popular or well-known media franchises, he got stung by YouTube's content-tagging algorithm. Intended to fight unauthorized uploads of copyrighted content, YouTube's technology scans newly uploaded videos to determine if they contain material that's been copyright-claimed by somebody else. If there's a match, the newly uploaded video can be blocked from the site entirely. This is what Nick says happened to him when he tried to do a Christmas special on the popular science fiction show *Black Mirror*. When he learned the video had been blocked, he decided to livestream it playing on his desktop as a way around the ban. He lasted for about twenty-five minutes, he says, before the livestream was shut down. "That hurt; that was an entire video lost," he said. "Even when you have the most positive things to say about mass media, the robots don't care."

Frustrated by YouTube's unpredictable system, he decided to try Patreon, a service that lets creators connect with—and receive money from—fans. During the Renaissance, influential families became patrons of the arts by financially supporting sculptors, painters, and other artists. Created in 2013 by a YouTube musician, Patreon is a small-scale, grassroots version of the same model. Fans of a particular creator pledge a certain number of dollars every month, and in exchange they get special benefits and (often) access to the creator. Patreon describes itself as a "win-win; creators retain creative freedom while getting the salary they deserve, and fans get to rest easy knowing that their money goes directly towards creating more of what they love." The site claims more than one hundred thousand creators and three million active monthly patrons.[2] Patreon takes a cut of what creators earn—between 5 and 12 percent of monthly income, depending on the creator's plan—as well as a payment processing fee.[3]

Nick spent a year creating his Patreon account, carefully creating and naming the various "tiers" of membership he'd offer. He decided on seven tiers, which run from the $1 a month Noctural Creature all the way up to a $50 a month Night Life Master option. When he set up his Patreon, he hoped to earn $800 a month through patrons, with a stretch goal of $1,200 a month. He said he met the second goal within six hours of his

Patreon page going live. "In an instant, it changed my life," he said. The steady income meant he could successfully focus on Night Mind full-time. But the new support also brought its own dilemma. Meeting his Patreon obligations, he said, involves a fair amount of "community upkeep." For example, even at the $1 tier, patrons get access to a Night Mind Discord. Creating a Discord means someone has to set up and moderate text and voice channels. He'd finally achieved his goal of going full-time as a YouTube creator, but he began to wonder if working on these community goals would leave him any time for the art that had attracted his patrons in the first place.

"Say you make those Patreon goals—are [patrons] really going to appreciate it as much as if you spent [time] on the content?" he asked. He liked Discord; it was a useful place to "drop information" about upcoming videos or to "hold court with the people who support you on the deepest level." But running it himself while also making videos was out of the question. He realized he would need to recruit others to help.

"When you're a person whose entire persona depends on your not showing your face, it's hard to find people to assist you in these matters whom you can trust," he said. He turned to his immediate circle. For his main admin, he recruited someone who'd been a part of his community for years, who showed up as a "kind face on Tumblr way back in the day" and was also one of Nick's first patrons. "When the Patreon opened, I recognized him immediately." When he asked his friend if he'd take the job—on a volunteer basis, of course—Nick says the response was an enthusiastic yes.

"He checks in every day," Nick said, and knows when to flag potential conflicts. Another one of the moderators? Nick's boyfriend, who "is an excellent mediator." Nick's philosophy is to keep your moderators close: "It's best when you're friends with the people who are the head of your community" because, he says, they know how you like to get things done.

The Night Mind Discord includes channels for a variety of topics, including "investigations," "puzzles and code-breaking," and something whimsically called "moonlight-garden." The description of this last channel is clearly written in Nick's voice:

> Welcome to the Garden! Most would call something like this a break room or lounge in other settings, but we keep it nocturnal here. This is a place reserved for conversations regarding whatever's on your mind—come take a walk, chat with those getting some air and moonlight, and come away feeling better to keep tackling fears, horrors, and all the rest. General is for general chatter, but a garden is for conversation of a nature that a good amount of moonlight, atmosphere, and some listening ears can most certainly help.

Other channel descriptions encourage visitors to "keep it kind" and "keep it spooky." His moderators know to report the biggest conflicts to him, although he also gets the occasional rant-y message from an unhappy community member. Many conflicts between community members aren't about Nick Nocturne, creepypasta content, or anything remotely related. They're "over the latest Pokémon game" or because "two personalities are [from] vastly different walks of life." Sometimes, people in his community will have a disagreement in an entirely different online area, but they'll bring it back to his Discord. He compared it to grade school: "You're the gym teacher. They had a fight in English class, but now they don't want you to pair them together."

He's bemused about it all. "This is so not what I signed up for or imagined happening, but that's the hard part. When you open yourself to having a community, you open the gate completely. Anybody who wants to walk in can do so."

The Discord server has been a site of interesting growth, both for Nick Nocturne and the community. He initially expected it would be like his Tumblr or Twitter, another "in character" space. Instead, it became a place to let his (cat) hair down:

> When you start the channel [and] you're wearing a mask all the time and people love that, you'd think that behind the scenes this is their chance to interact with you in character a bit more. Slowly you come to realize that a lot of the true-blue ones, who aren't just there to donate, they allow you to be human, to take off the mask. You can joke with them and play with them a bit. You can have a more relaxed atmosphere, you can giggle with the person who's making memes out of your content.

Discord and Patreon—where he has started posting exclusive patron-only videos—have helped Nick stay in touch with what he thinks of as his core community, something YouTube has actually inhibited. He says he sees a lot more off-topic posts, short posts, and negativity in his YouTube comments—people criticizing his voice, his editing style, or other choices. He refers to these critics as the "screaming minority," but they get to him. He wonders how to become more thick-skinned, or sometimes he goes into a "tailspin." At times like these, he's been encouraged by the community in his Discord:

> You've got the most heartfelt people, the ones who are paying money to help support your existence, who have seen you through all of it. You find out who the heart of your community really is and what they have to say, and it can really help bolster yourself.

He's also wandered into other creepypasta Discords, working collaboratively with fans there on cracking particularly challenging webseries. He says he's spent hours "mak[ing] sense of things, ask[ing] questions"—and these are the kinds of conversations he loves. When he does work with another community to find answers, he tries to credit them in the video he creates. This is partly his nature, but partly because so much of the ARG ethos is about collaboration.

Discord and Patreon have become successful, Nick said, in part because they offer creators more control and more intimacy with their communities. Discord, he said, has "done a great job" because they "morphed into a modern AIM"—the small-scale, more private chat service of yesteryear. YouTube, which he criticized for not being run by creators, hasn't prioritized building that type of community experience. The focus on subscriber counts and comment totals can hide the things that make communities rewarding—support, encouragement, loyalty.

He's spent a lot of time wondering why people feel more able to make negative remarks on his videos now that his channel is more successful, and he's landed on a simple explanation: "We equate giant numbers with faceless corporations. . . . The bigger you get, the less they see you as a person and the colder they feel they can be to you," he said, an observation that transcends social media, even though it's readily apparent there. "Numbers obscure humanity."

8.

Out of the Darkness

Kink and FetLife

In early 2017, Larry Nannery woke up and logged in to FetLife .com. This was nothing out of the ordinary—he'd been a member and frequent visitor to the site since 2010. He used the site to connect with others who shared his kinks; founded in 2008, FetLife is a social network where people connect around niche sexual fantasies. It's one of the largest such communities in the world: FetLife's public splash page says they have 8,311,588 members in 137,516 groups.[1] Or, as the page puts it, "Kinky heaven!" There are communities and groups for almost all possible fetishes: alongside things like BDSM (bondage, discipline, dominance, submission, and sadomasochism) and blindfolds, there are fetishes that might be less familiar to a non-kinky audience: smoking, PVC, and Tantra appear on the list.

The site's mission statement paints it as a safe, nonjudgmental haven for all types of kinksters: "To help people feel comfortable with who they are sexually by connecting and educating kinksters in a safe, open, and supportive environment."

The site's community guidelines also emphasize being "Open-Minded and Non-Judgemental":

> People often say to us how they love the fact that Fet-Life's community is so open-minded and non-judgemental, and we are proud of that. Please help us make sure Fet-Life stays this way. There is no place on here for any "my kink is ok but yours is not" attitude.

Since its founding, FetLife has become a key part of the kinky community, a place to see and be seen. Although other sites sprang up trying to do similar things, Larry said that "there's nothing close to FetLife in terms of depth and community." When he started using FetLife, he was no stranger to online communities. He'd met his first wife through an IRC online community for California. That group focused on "general life," not kinks, but as a self-identified introvert, he found he "was able to have a lot of expression online but not in person." It wasn't until his first marriage dissolved and he moved to New York that he started using the internet to find other kinky people. He started out in IRC chats and Yahoo groups, and eventually moved to FetLife not long after the site was created. At the time, the site, he said, felt very peer-to-peer, and "at the core just about anything went."

That all changed for him in early 2017. When he logged in, he noticed that several of his discussion posts and groups had disappeared without warning. In looking around the site, he saw that other users were in a similar bind. Larry says it was more than a week before site management, under pressure from the community, finally explained what had happened. FetLife founder John Baku uploaded a blog post in which he said that FetLife's credit card processors, citing vague concerns about edgy content like blood and "vampirism," had threatened to yank technical support from the site. Nervous about losing their ability to process credit card payments (membership dues from paying account holders make up part of FetLife's revenue, with the rest coming from advertising), the management team purged scores of groups and photos overnight, without any notice to users.

Some of Larry's posts were caught up in the purge. To Larry, it felt like his safe space had been yanked away, and his kink was being judged. To a kinkster, already a marginalized identity, this judgment felt both painful and scathing.

"To all of a sudden be told that my brain and what I do with my community is not acceptable, to a point where a credit card company thinks that I'm salacious or out of bounds, that was sobering," he said. Much of his content was later restored, but he stayed away from the site for years afterward.

It was neither the first nor the last time that something like this had happened. Depending on whom you ask, FetLife is an invaluable social network for kinksters, an educational resource about a marginalized identity, or a porn site for those with niche tastes. Because of its size and scope, FetLife has also been—unwillingly, if the founder's posts are anything to go by—on the front lines of ongoing controversies about how free we can be about sex on the internet. While FetLife may not be everyone's cup of tea—it is, after all, a site for people with non-mainstream sexual interests—it is also a community comprising, by their own policy, exclusively adults who have chosen to be there. But that doesn't mean they haven't been caught in the crosshairs of changing online regulations.

After the 2017 purges, FetLife management apologized for not giving users a warning, but emphasized that for financial, legal, and community reasons, the new content restrictions would remain, including ones against any material that fantasized about nonconsensual scenarios, impaired consent (such as by drugs or alcohol), or permanent physical damage (burning, very deep cutting). Many of these things, the site's management made clear, are legitimate fetishes, but also ones that banks get nervous about. In one blog post explaining the new guidelines and changes that were still to come, Baku painted a picture of what management faced:

> We live in a new world where, instead of having things like this play out in court to determine if something is lawful or not, what governmental and political organizations are doing is putting pressure on financial institutions, service providers, etc. to cut access to funds, critical services, etc. to get rid of things they don't like. After all, it's easier, faster, and cheaper for them to do that.
>
> I'm not saying that is what happened or that it's currently happening to us. I'm saying that this happens all the time, and it could easily happen to us. Sadly, we don't even know what happened in our case, nor do I think we will ever know.

Creating new community guidelines for FetLife was no easy task, as later community-facing blog posts made clear. The definition of a sex act varies from location to location, and so do laws around sexual expression. FetLife has numerous layers: private groups, public groups, personal profiles, and one-on-one messaging. The end result is a pastiche of changing regulations; in a more recent round of changes, for example, all visible blood was banned from the site's public pages. In theory, members had the chance to participate in some of these changes, although the participation process has also changed over the years.

In order to browse the site, an account is required; a real name is not (and in fact, many people use screen names). Signing up for FetLife doesn't require a photo, but it does require choosing a fetish or two. It also requires a real and verifiable phone number. Within the site, clicking on a section labeled Fetishes takes account holders to a page of hyperlinked keywords. Clicking on a keyword pulls up a page listing members and groups for that particular fetish. Clicking on one of these profiles offers its own pathway into the site: users can link to other site users whom they're in relationships with, upload photos, start groups, write posts, and send private messages.

There are two layers of conversation and moderation on FetLife. The first are the official community guidelines, which apply to everyone on the site. The second layer of guidelines comes from the site's volunteer moderators, who run the user-formed groups where community members find and talk with each other. Groups have been a key part of the FetLife universe almost since its founding. The largest of these—at nearly three hundred thousand members—is the Novices & Newbies group. It's the lobby that many newcomers pass through on their way into the site's maze of smaller communities and groups. According to Cowhideman,[2] who's been running the Novices & Newbies group for the past ten years, his moderation team hasn't been hugely affected by the high-level changes. If anything, partly because they deal with newcomers, they've often had to create stricter rules than the rest of the site as a whole.

"When we first instituted the rules, they were much stricter. FetLife had some appropriately waffle-y language about not sexualizing underage people. So when you're talking about the first time your friend tied you up when you were twelve, if you tell that matter-of-factly, you're not really sexualizing a twelve-year-old, you're telling your story," he said, by way of example. "We finally said 'No, we know what the FL rules are; these are ours.'" Members can't talk about *any* sexual experience involving a minor—even if it's a fantasy, even if the minor in question is themselves in the past. Occasionally, Cowhideman told me, users will push back with comments like "Where I live, the age of consent is sixteen." FetLife's management may have to contend with these changing local laws, but Cowhideman's response is: "We don't care if [the age of consent] is thirty-five." The group is a private space; the moderators get to decide. FetLife has since tightened site-wide guidelines around discussion of underage activity, Cowhideman says, probably "for a lot of the same reasons we found we were having trouble."

The group has six moderators—a vanishingly small number, considering its size. Cowhideman is the owner and the veteran.

The group's guidelines are extensive, and appear in multiple places. They read a little like the rules shouted by a frazzled counselor on the first day of summer camp. For example: "This is not a public soapbox. This is not a place to post your essays, your rants, or your personal journal"; "This group is not about getting you laid. For that, you're on your own"; or "Yet another policy we shouldn't have to have. No posts about killing people."

Here, as defined in several places, is what the group *is* for:

> Despite the name, this group is open to people with all levels of experience. The intention is to create a place where discussions on a wide variety of topics are conducted in ways that will be understandable to novices. Anyone discussing things here has to be prepared to understand that people may not understand all the vocabulary, people may have misconceptions about how kink works, and that not everyone is up to speed on what the common understandings of things might be.
>
> At the same time, it's a group for adults. If you don't understand something, ask. If someone else doesn't understand something, either explain or make your own point, but don't insult or be snarky with someone just because they seem not to know what you mean.

Cowhideman says it's a "disservice" to novices not to have a place like this, where they can go to ask questions. Some of the questions are specific to kink: newcomers wonder how open to be with friends and family, or how to get started with a particular fetish. Most questions get several thoughtful responses; some-times, the commenters start arguing with each other, at which point moderators jump in to referee.

"In other groups that aren't prepared for novices and new-bies, it's more of a system shock when they get a bunch of people who are brand-new," said Cowhideman. Not so for their group. When he took over the group's ownership, they had four thou-sand members, and moderators weren't sure how to handle what they then thought was an enormous size. The group has only grown since:

> We've got some nebulous number of people who are avid readers but never participate. We've got a core group of people who participate regularly, and then we've got a whole bunch of people who are committed to being part of it but who aren't there every day. It's kind of juggling all those sensibilities, and then on top of that we're all aware that we're a lot of people's entry point to the site and to kink and the community.

This is a large responsibility, and it's one that Cowhideman shoulders with apparent enthusiasm. Some of the tools the mod-erators have developed, such as prohibiting any discussion about underage sexual activity, are pragmatic solutions to common problems. But others involve making time for difficult conversations specific to the kink community: norms around safety, privacy, con-sent, hygiene, and mental health. The group is a place for discus-sion and education. No personal ads of any kind are allowed, and one of the moderators' all-caps admonishments, which appears in one of the lengthy guidelines posts, is "STOP HITTNG ON MEMBERS." The reason: "We choose to keep Novices & Newbies a safe space for new members to ask questions without getting hit on." There are plenty of other groups on FetLife for finding partners and playmates, and some of the work of Novices & Newbies involves directing newcomers to the right group.

Not surprisingly, in a group for newcomers, people often ask variations of the same question. Things like: "How do my partner and I open up our relationship?" "What's a safe word, and why should I use one?" "How do I use FetLife to find a group?" "What do you *really* think about *Fifty Shades of Grey?*"[3]

Not long ago, one of the group's moderators hit upon the idea of using a FetLife feature called "sticky posts" to pin frequently asked questions (and their answers) to the top of the forum's front page. These sticky posts include things like an introduction thread (the moderators don't recommend introducing yourself, partly because some people on the site will specifically hit on new members via private message, but people like to do it anyway); a note about how to get moderators' attention; and guides to reading lists, finding people, staying safe, and negotiating kink with "vanilla" (i.e., non-kinky) partners. Every time a particularly worthwhile discussion on one of these topics gets added, the moderators tag the discussion into a sticky post, which means the sticky posts are both set and constantly evolving. The whole collection constitutes "a really robust frequently asked questions section," said Cowhideman. Newcomers can read these posts, although Cowhideman ruefully acknowledged that many people don't. "The flip side of that is, when someone asks a very generic question, we can just point them to those," he said.

For example, moderators have an extensive set of sticky posts under the headline Staying Safe, Limits, Consent, Privacy & Health. Some of the most common questions focus on what consent means in the context of kinky relationships, especially BDSM, when one partner often takes on a submissive role or submits to painful activities like flogging, being burned with hot wax, or even being stuck with needles. Questions around ethical consent form the heart of many kink discussions, and have for years. Things like "What does consent really mean?" or "What do I have to put up with to get in the door?" appear often, Cowhideman said. In the introduction to the section on consent and staying safe, Cowhideman nods to why the discussion is so important, not just for the group but also for kinkster identity writ large:

> These topics generate some of the most debate in the community, some of it heated, some of it calmer, but many people consider them to be at the heart of what it is we do, and what separates BDSM from abuse and sociopathic behavior, so it isn't surprising that there are varied—and strong—opinions on the subjects.

Each of the conversations that's been tagged into the sticky posts comes from a debate that's actually happened, so readers can see the original question and the many responses it inspired. Clicking the top-line headline leads to an index, which includes headers for Safewords, Limits, Consent, and Negotiations, and

Health and Physical Safety Issues Relating to Play, to name a few. Each of these headers has a series of bullet points underneath. The bullet points under Health and Physical Safety include Kink and Mental Health, Bruising, Talking to the Doctor, and—cryptically—Bad Ideas. FetLife's formatting is idiosyncratic: the site background is black. Text is red, white, or gray, sometimes all caps, often hard to read. It's unclear whether the site's designers are in on a joke; at the end of the sidebar menu, an unusually tiny note in dark gray text reads: "If you can read this, you have really good eye sight!—John 4:69."

Clicking one of the capitalized headings leads to an expanded page. Each bullet point has hyperlinked discussions under it. Bad Ideas takes on alarming clarity, with links to discussions about experimenting with staples, stun guns, and tying someone up with an internet cable. It becomes apparent, reading through that last discussion, that there's a fine line between "dangerous in a sexy way" and just plain dangerous; the group exists so advanced practitioners can help newcomers stay on the right side of the line.

In another sticky-posted discussion, about safe words, a newcomer asks whether it's safe to engage in BDSM without a safe word. Dozens of thoughtful responses follow, the vast majority of them variations on the theme of "no," and including suggestions that newcomers, especially, should have clear ways of indicating their limits, whether that's a specific word or a general philosophy of communicativeness.

In another post, members debate whether a submissive poster's rights were violated when a partner didn't respond to a safe word in the expected way. This discussion involves a fair bit of back-and-forth. At one point, a mod interjects—with the phrase MOD NOTE appended to the top of their text in capital red letters—to indicate that a response was rude. Later on, the same mod intervenes—with the MOD NOTE text again—to break up a disagreement between two commenters. Cowhideman appears, but as a private citizen, no Mod Note header, to offer a paragraphs-long response, starting with the following:

> The most common understanding of a safe word, and, as much as there is any such thing in a community that doesn't have a governing body or a police force, the consensus for "how it works" is that unless something else is negotiated, the use of a safe word should stop everything immediately (with allowances made for safety—if something has to be done to stabilize the situation before things can safely stop, that's what's done).

Conversations about consent are some of the richest, but also the most challenging, in the group, Cowhideman says. A particular subset of consent known as consensual non-consent has a history of becoming so contentious that he now calls it an "impossible topic." Another impossible topic: cheating on a partner. In the context of this particular forum, infidelity comes up in the form of a newcomer asking what to do when their non-kinky partner doesn't want to or can't indulge their sexual desires. The group rules make it clear the group is not for advice about cheating.

The forum gets twenty to thirty new messages a day. In addition to creating the sticky posts, Cowhideman says most moderators have a Word document or two with common responses prewritten and ready to post. While Reddit moderators told me about using auto-moderator to help auto-populate common post replies, Cowhideman has built something similar for himself, using macros. He says there are "probably a dozen things we have to tell someone in one form or another every day," including answers to common questions like "I'm new. What do I do now?" He's written out replies for these common queries and situations, and with a keypress, he can post the canned response to the forum and direct the user to an existing discussion. The macro allows him to choose ways to frame the message; for example, "Your question is very general" or "This is a question that would be better in a different group for your local area." He has another macro that he uses to post prewritten responses directing people "to various group rules," and a few scripted messages to send to people who've insulted other members. Other moderators on his team, he says, have their own canned responses. When a new moderator joins, he shares his list, but tells them to use those as a starting point to write their own.

Cowhideman manages the group out of a sense of personal responsibility, a desire to pay it forward. Or, as the group description says, "We were all new once." As a gay leatherman in his late fifties (he turns sixty in 2020), Cowhideman remembers life before the internet. Back then, he told me, "leather" was a catchall term for kink in the gay community, and getting laid meant tracking down a gay bar. "My first date, I was twenty-eight years old and it was a felony," he said, which gives him some perspective when the occasional eighteen-year-old pops up on FetLife complaining about how hard it is to lose their virginity.

He started using AOL chat rooms to meet other gay men back in the 1990s, and remembers it as a sea change. "For gay people, it was one of the first opportunities to be part of a community that didn't involve going out after dark to often unsavory neighborhoods and staying out until two in the morning," he said.

The internet also provided a place to play with sexual identity and relationships. He created two separate AOL personas. "One was for me to write to my mom and get my emails and order stuff from wherever we ordered things from," he said. "The other was this fantasy image that I created that I knew I could never live up to." This is how "Cowhideman," as an identity, was born. (The username "Leatherman" was already taken.) His fantasy self was attractive, experienced, adventurous—a dream he thought would never come true, especially as a gay ex-military man living in a small town and late to the dating game. Shrouded in this identity, he would log in to chat rooms, where conversations often took place in secrecy:

> If you were just sitting and watching what was going on in the chatroom, someone would log in and say hi, and nothing would happen. So if you were just reading the chatroom, you'd be like "This is boring." But what would actually happen is that someone would come in and say hi, everyone would open their profile, and it would all be private messages. So the public face of the chatroom was utterly boring.

Behind the scenes, in private messages, is where "all bets were off, usually badly spelled and typing one-handed and all that." The same careful codes prevailed in online profiles: "AOL being what it was, your boss or your pastor could find your profile, so you didn't want your profile to be too obvious." He referred to the Hanky Code, a popular form of subtle messaging among gay leathermen in the 1970s: people wore differently colored handkerchiefs to signal what sexual fetishes they were looking for. When looking for partners moved online, so did the code. He'd scan the colors in people's profiles to figure out what they wanted. "You could just say red, yellow, polka dot, and lavender [in your profile]. Somebody reading along would go 'That's gotta be an ugly living room,' and someone else would be like 'That's cool, I gotta hook up with him.'"

Like a lot of early adopters, he soon moved from AOL into other online communities. For a while, he participated in a small kink-focused online discussion group run by a therapist. "It had a lot of great discussions. That's where I got my first taste of being a member of a community, where you were like 'Oh, there he is again' or 'There she is again.'" That community started winding down—it was hosted on a personal website, he said—and someone told him about FetLife. He wasn't one of the first users, but he was definitely early.

Over the years, he has seen the community grow dramatically. In the beginning, he said, the site largely grew through word of mouth, and many of the people there had been referred by someone else, or had already been in a kink community for a while. "Now the assumption is that every third person you run into is brand new," he said, which has raised interesting challenges for the group. When he first started moderating Novices & Newbies, they'd go months without banning anybody; now they ban as many as fifteen people in a day, usually for violating clearly spelled-out rules like the one against personal ads. At first the moderators felt bad about bringing down the banhammer, but now it's just another morning at the office.

Although they've become experts at handling newbies, they still face challenges when they get a sudden influx of new members—often from other sites that have been shut down. FetLife has persevered, even as the climate has gotten more difficult for online sex. In 2018, the government passed two regulations, called the Allow States and Victims to Fight Online Sex Trafficking Act, or FOSTA, and the Stop Enabling Sex Traffickers Act, or SESTA. The laws specified that online platforms could be held liable if they "promote and facilitate prostitution" or "facilitate traffickers in advertising the sale of unlawful sex acts with sex trafficking victims."[4] The law was intended to target sites that knowingly supported child sex trafficking, but critics said its broad wording made life more difficult for legitimate sex workers and sexual minorities.[5] Shortly after it became law, Craigslist announced that it would shut down its long-standing personals sections. The site's management issued a note, which is still up today: "Any tool or service can be misused. We can't take such risk without jeopardizing all our other services, so we have regretfully taken craigslist personals offline."[6]

Craigslist personals had been an essential meeting spot, especially for sexual minorities; Cowhideman refers to Craigslist personals as "everybody's singles bar for years." In the weeks before the shutdown, Craigslist commenters scanned the internet for alternatives, and some of them came to FetLife. Their arrival presented a cultural conflict. Craigslist personals were all about the hookup: explicit pics and brief messages were par for the course. FetLife had a whole different culture. "[On FetLife] you don't have the field where you say, 'I want people between five foot tall and five foot eight,'" Cowhideman said, by way of example. In fact, the FetLife community often resisted making the site more hookup-focused, on a principle Cowhideman describes as "enough horny idiots in my inbox as it is." Unfortunately, the number of horny idiots shot up. Personal ads appeared in groups that had long forbidden them; users were suddenly swamped with private messages. "We went from having to shut down a few carefully worded things to having to shut down twenty to thirty a day of 'Hi, I'm from Cleveland and six foot whatever and this is how I'm hung,'"[7] said Cowhideman. They were able to calm the storm, in part because they had honed their newcomer-handling skills over years of incremental group growth. Some of the new members stayed and learned FetLife's rules; others left.

Another, smaller wave happened around the release of the famed *Fifty Shades of Grey*, a fantasy novel about a sexually inexperienced young woman who gets into a submissive relationship with a wealthy man in his twenties. The book became a massive bestseller, and its subsequent movies brought the BDSM-curious to FetLife in droves. Many experienced kinksters view *Fifty Shades* with a wary eye. Emma Green, writing in the

Atlantic, summarized some of the complaints that have been leveled against the text:

> As several experienced BDSM practitioners emphasized to me, there are healthy, ethical ways to consensually combine sex and pain. . . . The problem is that *Fifty Shades* casually associates hot sex with violence, but without any of this context.[8]

Cowhideman says that most readers understood that *Fifty Shades* was an unrealistic fantasy (at least from a financial perspective!) and didn't arrive in the forum with requests like "I want to go on helicopter rides in my underwear."[9] But they did have questions about how to negotiate the boundaries of consent in kinky relationships, especially BDSM: primed by the book, they needed tutorials on ethical consent. Cowhideman says that experienced BDSM practitioners often found themselves repeating some variant of: "You [the submissive partner] can say no."

Over the years, he's developed a general sense of goodwill about much of the insanity that goes on in a group for newcomers, but there's one thing he still finds frustrating: when people don't read the rules, and then claim they shouldn't have to. More than five years ago, he gave vent to his pent-up frustration in a screed titled "Novices shouldn't have to read or obey the rules of a group called Novices & Newbies, because they're new. Even though they are adults. Because they're new."

Intended as a no-holds barred response to the (unidentified) entitled newbie, the post begins with the following:

Okay, so you're new, you're eager, you're confused, and the site isn't set up the way most of them are. We can relate. We didn't design the site either, and we were all new here once, too. It's not particularly intuitive. We get that.

So when it's an honest mistake and we point it out, and it's "oops" and "it won't happen again" then, usually, no harm no foul and welcome to the group. Really. Mistakes happen. And if we weren't prepared to deal with confused and disoriented people, we wouldn't be involved in a group called Novices & Newbies.

But when you climb into our inboxes and call us Nazis, threaten to sue, proclaim that we are violating your First Amendment Rights, or send us an oh-so-earnest butt-hurt diatribe about how you're so new, and that novices shouldn't have to follow rules because, well, they're new, and we should waive the rules for them, in a group called Novices & Newbies, and then start calling us names, well, you know, it's annoying.

And yes, all of that has happened. And yes, all of it has happened THIS WEEK. It pretty much happens EVERY week.

The post was intended, he says, as "self-defense." He was fed up with people climbing into his inbox and calling him a fascist for deleting their personal ad; he'd reached a point of such frustration that he needed to let off steam or quit moderating entirely. The post resonated. It now has almost twenty-four thousand responses—many of them variations on "Thank goodness you said it." Over time, it's become a general venting space. Other moderators sometimes wander into the thread to share egregious examples of behavior from their own forums, provided no one is identifiable, of course. Moderators on the Novices & Newbies team use it to commiserate. Cowhideman notes that it's taken some wacky detours: at one point, they deviated from discussions of moderator angst to debate the merits of vegan haggis and Lady Godiva.

The thread taught him an important lesson about moderation, which is that "there has to be a mechanism for blowing off steam, because it's not a job. I suppose things would be different in a paid situation, but when it's volunteers and a labor of love, it's so easy to get overwhelmed." Many of the moderators I spoke to for this book talked about back channels for moderator communication, which included special inboxes, forums, and Facebook groups. A lot of these tools help moderators work better, but Cowhideman went a step further and talked about how important it was for moderators to bond *outside* the context of their moderation work. He compared the "blowing off steam" thread to a more corporate cousin: the team lunch. All of these activities are a way of creating what he described as a "group identity" that goes beyond the daily minutiae of the job at hand. The thread is a way for the moderators to have a little fun together; and these occasional in-jokes make his volunteer moderation team possible.

He no longer wants to quit moderating, but he also doesn't imagine doing it forever. He told me he's "aged out" of a lot of community kinky things. He's married and somewhat settled down (sometimes, when people ask how he learned about FetLife, he jokes, "My mother-in-law told me [about it]"). A little while ago, he went back and looked at the unrealizable fantasy identity he created for himself decades ago when he first started meeting men online. He was struck, he said, by how "tame" that identity now feels, like "That's a Tuesday." Apparently fantasies do come true; FetLife has been one part of that journey.

He doesn't know what future FetLife has as a site, either. That's not just because of increasing legal crackdowns on online sex. He sees that FetLife is becoming an institution, and institutions have "shelf lives." He's seen it happen to the gay leather bar. There was a time when gay leather bars were "critical to the central social life." They're still around, but they don't have that role anymore, he said, thanks in part to the unprecedented social shifts enabled by the internet and the cell phone. Mores change, too—when Cowhideman's grandmother was born, "only prostitutes showed their ankles in public." He can envision a future in which kink is mainstream. The trend of meeting romantic partners online may be a blip, or it may prove enduring. People will always want to connect, but maybe they'll find other ways of doing it. "The next generation are going to tell their grandparents 'they've come up with this brand new thing where you go to a club and you don't know anybody but you just show up and you dance and it's an amazing cutting-edge thing and you don't have to do it online anymore,'" he hypothesized with a laugh. "FetLife will inevitably become what the frumpy old people do."

Conclusion

I loved every minute of writing this book, and I hope you enjoyed at least some of reading it. Community moderators touch every part of our online experience, all the time.

Despite their power and their diligence, community moderators are not a panacea for a broken internet. No single moderator has that kind of power, and there's no one magical online community where everyone will get along or be nice to one another. Community moderators intentionally work with limited sets of people. Their hardest decisions aren't about which comment to include and which to exclude but rather about whom their spaces are for. Does the queer gamer get to have a say? In discussions about racism, should people who have experienced its negative effects get more consideration? If so, how does that reconcile with other participants' right to a point of view? If you activate an online mob, how do you deal with the fallout when that mob is less than polite, or when they're accused of stifling conversation?

No matter how thoughtful moderators are, they can't make everyone happy. Reseph's *Final Fantasy XIV* subreddit hosted long conversations between moderators and disaffected community members. Many of their disagreements involved questions with no objectively right answer: *Should* a forum allow fanart? What qualifies as a self-promotional post? When moderators make decisions about these types of things, they change who enters the community. To the extent that community moderators can help mend a broken internet, it's piece by piece, and only for select communities. Even within these curated and chosen communities, there will still be contests over who has the right to speak, and where, and when, and for how long.

But that's what makes online moderation interesting. It says something about the internet we want, but also about the internet we're willing to build. It takes effort, foresight, experience, and technical acumen to create online communities. This work begins long before shutting off comments on an angry thread. It happens when moderators sit down, like Justine and Tria did at MADA, and intentionally decide which emoji should represent a cry for help, and how moderators should respond to it. That's partly why community moderation requires humans, at least for the foreseeable future.

It's surprising, now, that we once believed platforms like Facebook had no moderators. Not only does Facebook have content moderators who remove legally objectionable and morally offensive content but they also have a wide army of community moderators who create a lot of the groups that keep people coming back to the site. YouTube depends on creators—an increasingly professionalized group—to power engagement, while Discord depends on gamers to set up and manage servers. The work and the services are inextricably intertwined. Many people have talked about how the relationship between platforms and moderators is exploitative, but that's too glib a take; many of the moderators I spoke to felt empowered, visible, and happy to be doing the work. Of course, some also felt resentful, underappreciated, underpaid, and justifiably frustrated when enormous profits went to someone else. Approaches like those of Patreon, which allows fans to donate directly to creators, and Ko-fi, a service that lets people tip their moderators, partly subvert the power of enormous platforms like YouTube and Facebook, but they do it by building more, different platforms.

Each group of moderators in this book offers a different set of lessons on how to approach online community. In the first chapter, the moderators of Make America Dinner Again have different political affiliations but are united by a desire to build bridges and by a singular sense of civic mission. They tried to thoughtfully adapt offline social norms to online behavior. MADA serves as a rebuttal to the idea that the internet is inherently dehumanizing, or that it's impossible to build empathy in a comments section. But to get there, MADA moderators spend hours framing controversial discussions, encouraging both light and heavy conversations, and building connections with members one at a time. Despite their hard work, it's impossible to extrapolate from one Facebook group to an entire nation: while MADA can offer some insight into how to frame political conversations among those who disagree, it can't be the only solution.

The moderators at Real Talk and Pantsuit Nation, on the other hand, take a different approach to difficult conversations.

The moderators of Real Talk have a clear point of view: they want to talk about anti-racism and restorative justice from an action-oriented perspective. Their platform is a space devoted to women of color, but they include others who are willing to listen to and learn from their perspective. They want to teach people how to confront their objectionable relatives at Thanksgiving dinner, and they see donations as a way to redress past social wrongs. In order to better achieve their goals, moderators have made extensive use of Facebook's platform—sometimes hacking it in clever ways—to create a divided "house," a place where discussions are fractured in order to eventually be made whole. This intentional separation allows difficult discussions to happen productively, because other, earlier conversations have taken place in "prep" parts of the house. Real Talk's anti-racist training demonstrates how to have a very tough conversation in a medium that isn't known for it.

The same is true for Pantsuit Nation, even though their moderators are working with a vast—and vastly different—group. Grace's experiences demonstrate how to try to bring an educator's philosophy to a big group with different goals and history.

The neighborhood moderators, meanwhile, have the opposite challenge: they're trying to build communal awareness among people who will *definitely* see each other offline. In a time when many people bemoan not knowing their neighbors, the neighborhood LISTSERV is a surprisingly intimate space; people reveal all aspects of themselves, accusing their neighbors of crimes one minute and exposing their own biases the next. But it's also a place where community identity—or part of it, anyway—is formed and commemorated. Many people seem to remember Peggy Robin's jokes in the Cleveland Park LISTSERV. Although it's not a traditional neighborhood group, NUMTOT is a fascinating entry in this space: its many spin-offs demonstrate how group identity can shift over time, and how breaking up can sometimes be part of staying together. Juliet's experiences as a modern media influencer demonstrate both the pros and cons of becoming famous for something you did in college. It's also a group for young people on Facebook, which is becoming increasingly rare as that platform's audience ages. The Sacramento Sister Circle has combined online community with offline activism, providing a space for its members to gather, discover shared concerns, and put pressure on local businesses.

Then there's Sleeping Giants—a concern essentially born of the internet. Their entire goal is to take on the rise of right-wing media, a rise that's partly fueled by a boom in programmatic advertising. But it's hard to make programmatic advertising interesting to the masses, so they've found a way to reduce the complex issue to a simple, appealing activist slogan. They've developed an arsenal of tools, including ways to target and activate people on both Twitter and Facebook, that—much like programmatic advertising itself—aren't bound by national identity. Doxxing is one of the risks and the horrors of being a public figure online, and Matt's story demonstrates how it can change someone's life—for better and for worse.

People who run online role-playing game communities, on the other hand, are interested in fun. And yet despite the fact that many gamers revere "fun," it turns out that running a gaming guild is an enormous amount of work. From gathering raid supplies to setting up Discord servers to getting on voice chat to navigating complex issues of identity, these communities tackle it all, sometimes to the exhaustion of their moderating crew. Of all the people I spoke to, these communities were active on the most "fronts"—that is, on the most platforms. They'd hang out in the game, with informal leaders taking ownership of individual sessions; they'd hang out in Discord chat, sending one another messages and memes in between gaming sessions; and they'd gather in voice chat during shared gaming. There's something surreal and immersive about hearing someone's voice over the phone while being in a game with them at the same time. In one particular game, *World of Warcraft*, collaborative groups anchor the gameplaying experience for frequent players. At the same time, Lee's experience as a moderator demonstrates that there is always space for new guilds, and that a hobby built around fun still intersects constantly with players' offline realities.

Reddit, one of the most famous online community sites in the world, has an elaborate and often controversial moderation apparatus, in which experienced moderators often mod multiple forums. The Reddit forum I investigated had job applications for moderators, open voting on new mods, and multiple ways for readers to offer feedback. Reseph spoke to me often about transparency, a reflection perhaps both of Reddit's public structure (anyone can view Reddit comments) and an awareness that members sometimes feel that moderation decisions are made in secret. There's a tension on Reddit between what non-moderators can and can't see, and between what moderators owe the community and vice versa. Reseph has used Reddit- and user-created tools to manage what he refers to as a near-perpetual "Eternal September"—an uneasy balance between old community members and new.

There's a popular perception that YouTube comments are the most obnoxious on the internet, save for online news and chan sites. So how do creators, who build their livelihoods on YouTube, manage to make it feel personal and nontoxic? Nick Nocturne of the creepypasta channel Night Mind talked about how the toxicity of comments scaled up along with his community, and is honest about the negative toll these comments took on him. As he gained followers, he turned to other platforms, including Patreon, to forge a more direct and paid relationship with fans. But these services required building special benefits for paying patrons. Many of these benefits revolved around access to Nick himself. Making this leap created, in effect, multiple Night Mind communities: those who watch on YouTube, those who pay, those who participate in paid Discord, and those who do some combination. All of these people know Nick differently, and they've experienced different sides of his online persona. He constantly wrestles with how much to let different audiences behind the Nick Nocturne mask. Many of his members meet one another in other creepypasta and ARG creator Discords dedicated to the hobby. He's gone into a few himself when he needed help cracking a particularly complex puzzle. At times like that, the line between "Nick Nocturne the online host" and "Nick Nocturne the person who likes ARGs" starts to blur.

And then, of course, there's online kink. FetLife, Craigslist, and scores of similar sites have transformed life for many people who identify with a niche sexual identity. To its members, FetLife is a gathering place, a site for shared and negotiated identity, and an expressive and emotional outlet. That's probably why members care about the site's policies, and why any decision about what is and is not acceptable—or legal—can lead to long discussions and disagreements. Cowhideman is a fascinating moderator—someone who freely admits he's too old for a lot of kinky hijinks but maintains his moderator role as a connection to the community. His group handles waves of newcomers that ebb and flow like tides. They've pulled together a series of hacks and valuable lessons for any moderator on how to deal with an influx of newbies and the challenges it presents to site culture. Hint: Keep guidelines clear, repeat them often, and assume that no one reads them anyway. Then make sure the moderators have a place where they can blow off steam.

These communities succeed—or at least continue to engage members—because their moderators generally know who and what they want. They also understand how to structure shifts, assign roles, manage responsibility, and release tension, regardless of whether they're paid to moderate or not. All of this work requires constant vigilance and care. Good moderators seem to have two common traits: a genuine interest in other people, and excellent communication skills. Both, it turns out, are essential to making an online community thrive. So is a certain willingness to accept the ways in which groups challenge individuals, or, as Justine of MADA put it, "Conflict is part of being a moderator. We have to be prepared to confront our own negative emotions and put them aside."

And it could all be gone tomorrow. Online communities come and go. Juliet talks about shutting down NUMTOT, in which case something else will spring up to take its place. Cowhideman thinks that it's FetLife's fate to become "frumpy," especially if kink becomes more mainstream. But the lessons these moderators have shared will continue to inform how we build relationships with one another in a world where online connection increasingly dominates how we meet, work, play, and love.

Acknowledgments

I have so many people to thank. This book would not be possible without them. I'm grateful to Sam Ford, for being such an excellent friend and advisor, and for believing in my work even before I did. He made all this possible by showing my master's thesis to the rest of the team at Tiller Press. I also want to thank Sam's spectacular team at Tiller. Michael Andersen, in particular, read early chapters of this book and provided references, suggestions, and general enthusiasm. My fantastic editor at Tiller Press, Emily Carleton, was patient and kind as I learned the publishing process, and her suggestions materially improved this manuscript.

I must thank my immediate family—Dad, Mom, Trisha, and Andrew. I'm grateful to Mom and Dad for endless cups of tea, and for their suggestions on early drafts of these chapters. Trisha talked me through several meltdowns with her extraordinary good sense, and made space for this book in her very crowded life. Andrew devoured every chapter I sent his way, and happily shared anecdotes and ideas from his own (extensive) experience in online communities.

My friends Seth Wiener and Carmel Arikat lent me their lawyerly expertise when I negotiated the book contract. The brilliant

An Xiao Mina gave me great suggestions—and a much-needed shot of confidence—in the form of suggestions on an early draft. My friends Kyrie Caldwell and Lacey Lord served as a sounding board for just about every idea I had, and also read and offered feedback on early chapters. My friend Andrew Phelps took my author photo, spending several hours capturing and editing the perfect shot. My friend Nate Matias talked with me about this project, pointed me toward resources, and connected me to others in the field.

As a journalist and researcher, I have a lot of friends who've written books, and I turned to some of them when I first started down this road. I'm grateful to An, Emily Goligoski, Caroline Kitchener, and my former *Atlantic* colleague Alexis Madrigal for their thoughtful suggestions about agents and contracts and their open, honest reflections on how they negotiated these things themselves.

Many of my friends offered constant emotional support. Their names and acts of kindness were so numerous that I don't have space to list them all here, but I'm incredibly grateful to have so many generous, caring people in my life. You keep me going.

At several points, I drew on the work and insights I compiled while writing my master's thesis. I'm so grateful to Matt Carroll for being a kind, generous advisor—and such a great friend and role model—then and now, and to the team at MIT CMS for giving me space to first explore these ideas.

Finally, I'm grateful to every one of the moderators and community members I spoke to for this book. I'm truly inspired by the care, generosity, and thoughtfulness you bring to your communities, and I hope I've done an all-right job representing that effort here. Thank you for introducing me to new worlds, and for enabling what—for me—was the most enjoyable part of this process.

The best parts of this story owe a debt to others; the mistakes are all mine.

Works Consulted

An expanded list of works I consulted in the process of writing this book.

2010–2014 ACS 5-Year Estimates Ward 3, Office of Planning, August 9, 2016, https://planning.dc.gov/node/1180945, ACS data for Ward 3.

"About FOSTA," Craigslist, https://www.craigslist.org/about/FOSTA.

"About Nextdoor Leads," Nextdoor, https://help.nextdoor.com/s /article/About-Nextdoor-Leads?language=en_US.

"About Us," Nextdoor, https://about.nextdoor.com/gb/.

Activision Blizzard, Inc., "Activision Blizzard Announces Record Fourth Quarter and Full Year Earnings Per Share," investor news release, February 5, 2015, https://investor.activision.com /static files/31066916-9fc0-49bf-9914-553661592dee.

Ahler, Douglas J. "Self-Fulfilling Misperceptions of Public Polarization." Journal of Politics 76, no. 3 (2014): 607–20; doi:10.1017/s0022381614000085.

Alter, Alexandra. "A Book Deal for Pantsuit Nation, and Then a Backlash." New York Times, December 21, 2016, https://www

.nytimes.com/2016/12/21/business/a-book-deal-for-pantsuit
-nation-and-then-a-backlash.html.

Barrett, Ben. "1,960 Man-Hours per Week: The Truth about *WoW*
Raiding at the Highest Level." *PCGamesN*, https://www
.pcgamesn.com/world-of-warcraft/wow-raiding-nighthold
-method-danish-terrace-death-jesters.

Beck, Julie. "The Concept Creep of 'Emotional Labor.'" *Atlantic*,
November 26, 2018, https://www.theatlantic.com/family
/archive/2018/11/arlie-hochschild-housework-isnt-emotional
-labor/576637/.

Bhattarai, Abha. "Breitbart Lost 90 Percent of Its Advertisers in
Two Months: Who's Still There?" *Washington Post*, June 8, 2017,
https://www.washingtonpost.com/news/business
/wp/2017/06/08/breitbart-lost-90-percent-of-its-advertisers
-in-two-months-whos-still-there/.

Bilton, Ricardo. "The *Wall Street Journal*'s New Tool Gives a Side-
by-Side Look at the Facebook Political News Filter Bubble."
NiemanLab, May 18, 2016, https://www.niemanlab.org/2016
/05/the-wall-street-journals-new-tool-gives-a-side-by-side
-look-at-the-facebook-political-news-filter-bubble/.

"Blue Feed, Red Feed." *Wall Street Journal*, last updated August 19,
2019, http://graphics.wsj.com/blue-feed-red-feed/.

Bolton, Kerra L. "Stephon Clark's Tweets Are a Reminder:
#SayHerName." CNN, April 19, 2018, https://www.cnn
.com/2018/04/19/opinions/stephon-clark-tweets-hurt
-women-bolton-opinion/index.html.

Borchers, Callum. "'Can You Name One White Nationalist Article at
Breitbart?' Challenge Accepted!" *Washington Post*, November
15, 2016, https://www.washingtonpost.com/news/the-fix

/wp/2016/11/15/can-you-name-one-white-nationalist-article-at
-breitbart-challenge-accepted/.

Braun, Joshua A., John D. Coakley, and Emily West. "Activism,
Advertising, and Far-Right Media: The Case of Sleeping
Giants." *Media and Communication* 7, no. 4 (December 2019):
68–79; doi:10.17645.

Breitbart News. "#Dumpkelloggs: Breakfast Brand Blacklists
Breitbart, Declares Hate for 45,000,000 Readers." Breitbart,
November 30, 2016, https://www.breitbart.com/politics
/2016/11/30/dumpkelloggs-kelloggs-declares-hate-45-million
-americans-blacklisting-breitbart/.

Breitbart Tech. "Would You Rather Your Child Had Feminism or
Cancer?" Breitbart, February 19, 2016, https://www.breitbart
.com/clips/2016/02/19/would-you-rather-your child-had
-feminism-or-cancer/.

Bromwich, Jonah Engel. "Can Society Scale?" *New York Times*,
August 10, 2018, https://www.nytimes.com/2018/08/10/style
/numtot-urbanism-memes.html.

Butler, Brian, Lee Sproull, Sara Kiesler, and Robert Kraut.
"Community Effort in Online Groups: Who Does the Work
and Why?" in Susan Weisband, ed., *Leadership at a Distance:
Research in Technologically-Supported Work*. New York:
Lawrence Erlbaum Associates, 2008.

"Cannes Lions: Social & Influence Winners 2019." Contagious, June
19, 2019, https://www.contagious.com/news-and-views/cannes
-lions-winners-2019-social-influencer-category.

Captain, Sean. "Disqus Grapples with Hosting Toxic Comments on
Breitbart and Extreme-Right Sites." *Fast Company*, March 8,
2017, https://www.fastcompany.com/3068698/disqus

-grapples-with-hosting-toxic-comments-on-breitbart-and
-extreme-right-sites.

Caruso, Justin. "'Non-Political' Sleeping Giants Repeatedly Go
after Steve King, Endorse Democrat Opponent." Breitbart,
October 24, 2018, https://www.breitbart.com/tech/2018/10/24
/non-political-sleeping-giants-repeatedly-go-after-steve-king
-endorse-democrat-opponent/.

Chalermkraivuth, Panchalay. "'She Can Lead. She Can Live.'
Black Women's March Draws Hundreds to State Capitol."
Sacramento Bee, June 22, 2019, https://www.sacbee.com/news
/local/article231865683.html.

Chamberlain, Libby, ed. *Pantsuit Nation*. New York: Flatiron Books, 2017.

Chen, Adrian. "Unmasking Reddit's Violentacrez, the Biggest Troll on
the Web." *Gawker*, October 12, 2012, https://www.gawker
.com/5950981/unmasking-reddits-violentacrez-the-biggest
-troll-on-the-web.

Chen, Adrian. "When the Internet's 'Moderators' Are Anything But."
New York Times Magazine, July 21, 2015, https://www.nytimes
.com/2015/07/26/magazine/when-the-internets-moderators
-are-anything-but.html.

"Crime or Suspicious Activity." Nextdoor, https://help.nextdoor
.com/s/article/be-helpful-not-hurtful?language=en_US#5.

Dosono, Bryan, and Bryan Semaan. "Moderation Practices as
Emotional Labor in Sustaining Online Communities: The Case
of AAPI Identity Work on Reddit." *CHI '19: Proceedings of
the 2019 CHI Conference on Human Factors in Computing
Systems*, paper no. 142, May 2019, https://dl.acm.org/citation
.cfm?id=3300372.

Fisher, Lauren. "US Programmatic Ad Spending Forecast 2019." Emarketer.com, April 25, 2019, https://www.emarketer.com /content/us-programmatic-ad-spending-forecast-2019.

Florida, Richard. "Young People's Love of Cities Isn't a Passing Fad." CityLab, May 28, 2019, https://www.citylab.com /life/2019/05/urban-living-housing-choices-millennials-move -to-research/590347/.

Fraser, Nancy. "Rethinking the Public Sphere: A Contribution to the Critique of Actually Existing Democracy." *Social Text* 25/26 (January 1, 1990): 56–80.

Gillespie, Tarleton. *Custodians of the Internet: Platforms, Content Moderation, and the Hidden Decisions That Shape Social Media.* New Haven, CT: Yale University Press, 2018.

Green, Emma. "Consent Isn't Enough: The Troubling Sex of *Fifty Shades.*" *Atlantic*, February 10, 2015, https://www.theatlantic .com/entertainment/archive/2015/02/consent-isnt-enough-in -fifty-shades-of-grey/385267/

Gruzd, Anatoliy, Barry Wellman, and Yuri Takhteyev. "Imagining Twitter as an Imagined Community." *American Behavioral Scientist* (July 25, 2011), https://journals.sagepub.com/doi /abs/10.1177/0002764211409378.

Grynbaum, Michael M., and John Herrman. "Breitbart Rises from Outlier to Potent Voice in Campaign." *New York Times*, August 26, 2016, https://www.nytimes.com/2016/08/27/business /media/breitbart-news-presidential-race.html.

Gupta, Anika. "Towards a Better Inclusivity: Online Comments and Community at News Organizations." Masters dissertation, Massachusetts Institute of Technology, 2016.

Harris, Ronan. "Improving Our Brand Safety Controls." *Google* (blog), March 17, 2017, https://blog.google/topics/google -europe/improving-our-brand-safety-controls/.

Horowitz, Juliana Menasce, Anna Brown, and Kiana Cox. "Race in America 2019." Pew Research Center, April 9, 2019, https://www .pewsocialtrends.org/2019/04/09/race-in-america-2019/.

IAB Europe. "The Current State of the Programmatic Advertising Market." *IAB Europe* (blog), March 21, 2019, https://iabeurope .eu/blog/the-current-state-of-the-programmatic-advertising -market.

Iyengar, Shanto, Yphtach Lelkes, Matthew Levendusky, Neil Malhotra, and Sean J. Westwood. "The Origins and Consequences of Affective Polarization in the United States." *Annual Review of Political Science* 22, no. 1 (May 11, 2019): 129–46; https://www-annualreviews-org.proxyau.wrlc.org /doi/10.1146/annurev-polisci-051117-073034.

Jacobs, Jane, Paul Kuhne, and C. J. Peek. "Participant-Identified Effects of Better Angels Experiences." October 2019, https:// drive.google.com/file/d/1kkpwt59p7Ci6jhtOaAlYFr0cqy4Q OAy9/view.

Jammi, Nandini. "PPC Marketers: Don't Wait for Permission to Blacklist Breitbart News." *Medium*, November 23, 2016, https:// www.medium.com/@nandoodles/ppc-marketers-dont-wait-for -permission-to-blacklist-breitbart-news-83872c2a7442.

Jenkins, Henry. "Video Games Myths Revisited: New Pew Study Tells Us about Games and Youth." *Confessions of an Aca-Fan* (blog), October 2, 2008, http://www.henryjenkins.org /blog/2008/10/video_games_myths_revisited_ne.html.

Jiang, Jialun "Aaron." "Voice-Based Communities and Why It's So Hard to Moderate Them." *ACM CSCW* (blog), *Medium*, August 29, 2019, https://www.medium.com/acm-cscw/voice -based-communities-and-why-they-are-so-hard-to-moderate -b3339c1f0f6a.

Jiang, Jialun "Aaron," Charles Kiene, Skylar Middler, Jed. R. Brubaker, and Casey Fiesler. "Moderation Challenges in Voice-Based Online Communities on Discord." *Proceedings of the ACM on Human-Computer Interaction* 3, no. CSCW, article 55 (November 2019), https://www.aaronjiang.me/assets /bibliography/pdf/cscw2019-discord.pdf.

Kelly, Heather. "Mark Zuckerberg Explains Why He Just Changed Facebook's Mission." CNN Money, June 22, 2017, https:// money.cnn.com/2017/06/22/technology/facebook-zuckerberg -interview/index.html.

Killian, Andrew. "What's Driving Growth in Urban Planning Degrees?" Data USA, April 3, 2016, https://www.datausa.io /story/04-04-2016_urban-planning-degrees.

Lewis, Harry. "Pantsuit Nation Is a Sham." *HuffPost*, December 20, 2016, https://www.huffpost.com/entry/panstuit-nation-is-a -sham_b_585991dce4b04d7df167cb4d.

Levine, Peter. "How to Respond?" November 11, 2016. http://www .peterlevine.ws/images/Screen-Shot-2016-11-11-at-1.19.30 PM-1.png.

Lo, Claudia. "When All You Have Is a Banhammer: The Social and Communicative Work of Volunteer Moderators." Masters dissertation, Massachusetts Institute of Technology, 2018.

Lynch, Brian, and Courtney Swearingen. "Why We Shut Down Reddit's 'Ask Me Anything' Forum." *New York Times*, July 8, 2015,

https://www.nytimes.com/2015/07/08/opinion/why-we-shut
-down-reddits-ask-me-anything-forum.html.

Maheshwari, Sapna. "Revealed: The People Behind an Anti-Breitbart
Twitter Account." *New York Times*, July 20, 2018, https://www
.nytimes.com/2018/07/20/business/media/sleeping-giants
-breitbart-twitter.html.

Margonelli, Lisa. "Inside AOL's 'Cyber-Sweatshop.'" *Wired*, October 1,
1999, https://www.wired.com/1999/10/volunteers/.

Marie, Jenina. "Open Letter to Pantsuit Nation." *Smart Media Mom*
(blog), December 3, 2016, https://smartmediamom
.com/2016/12/03/open-letter-to-pantsuit-nation/.

Masden, Christina, Catherine Grevet, Rebecca Grinter, Eric Gilbert,
and W. Keith Edwards. "Tensions in Scaling-Up Community
Social Media: A Multi-Neighborhood Study of Nextdoor."
https://www.cc.gatech.edu/~keith/pubs/nextdoor-chi2014.pdf.

Matias, J. Nathan. "Preventing Harassment and Increasing Group
Participation through Social Norms in 2,190 Online Science
Discussions." *PNAS* 116, no. 20 (May 14, 2019); https://www.pnas
.org/content/pnas/116/20/9785.full.pdf.

Mayyasi, Alex. "The AOL Chat Room Monitor Revolt." *Priceonomics*,
August 21, 2014, https://www.priceonomics.com/the-aol-chat
-room-monitor-revolt/.

McCoy, Terence. "Georgetown Social Network Accused of Racial
Profiling Is Suspended." *Washington Post*, October 19, 2015,
https://www.washingtonpost.com/local/georgetown
-social-network-accused-of-racial-profiling-is-suspended
/2015/10/19/7a8865a2-7674-11e5-b9c1-f03c48c96ac2_story
.html.

Medina, Jennifer. "Website Meant to Connect Neighbors Hears Complaints of Racial Profiling." *New York Times*, May 18, 2016, https://www.nytimes.com/2016/05/19/us/website-nextdoor-hears-racial-profiling-complaints.html.

Michelle, Lecia. "Nonblack POC, Stop Acting Like Black Women Are Invincible and Don't Feel Pain." *Medium*, June 18, 2018, https://www.medium.com/@LeciaMichelle/nonblack-poc-stop-acting-like-black-women-are-invincible-and-dont-feel-pain-803970064ef4.

Michelle, Lecia. "White Women Can't Even Commit to a 2-Week Racial Justice Mentoring Class." *Medium*, November 25, 2018, https://www.medium.com/@LeciaMichelle/white-women-cant-even-commit-to-a-2-week-racial-justice-mentoring-class-fd58049d3633.

Milo. "Gawker: 'Dishonest Fascists' of GamerGate Could Cost Us 'Millions.'" Breitbart, October 23, 2014, https://www.breitbart.com/europe/2014/10/23/gawker-dishonest-fascists-of-gamergate-could-cost-us-millions.

Mina, An Xiao. *Memes to Movements: How the World's Most Viral Media Is Changing Social Protest and Power*. Boston: Beacon Press, 2019.

Mostrous, Alexi. "Big Brands Fund Terror through Online Adverts." *The Times*, February 9, 2017, https://www.thetimes.co.uk/article/big-brands-fund-terror-knnxfgb98.

Newton, Casey. "Bodies in Seats." *Verge*, June 19, 2019, https://www.theverge.com/2019/6/19/18681845/facebook-moderator-interviews-video-trauma-ptsd-cognizant-tampa.

Newton, Casey. "The Trauma Floor: The Secret Lives of Facebook Moderators in America." *Verge*, February 25, 2019, https://www

.theverge.com/2019/2/25/18229714/cognizant-facebook
-content-moderator-interviews-trauma-working-conditions
-arizona.

Ng, David. "Chick-fil-A Will Stop Donating to Salvation Army,
Christian Athletes Following LGBT Pressure." Breitbart,
November 18, 2019, https://www.breitbart.com/tech/2019
/11/18/chick-fil-a-will-stop-donating-to-salvation-army
-christian-athletes-following-lgbt-pressure/.

"Partisanship and Political Animosity in 2016." Pew Research Center,
June 22, 2016, https://www.people-press.org/2016/06/22
/partisanship-and-political-animosity-in-2016/.

Pearson, Jordan. "Yahoo Groups Is Winding Down and All Content
Will Be Permanently Removed." Vice, October 16, 2019, https://
www.vice.com/en_us/article/8xwe9p/yahoo-groups-is-winding
-down-and-all-content-will-be-permanently-removed.

Perez, Maria. "Steve Bannon Out at Breitbart: Seven Most
Controversial Articles Published by Trump's Former Aide."
Newsweek, January 9, 2018, https://www.newsweek.com
/steve-bannon-breitbart-trump-controversial-776262.

Peters, Jay. "Yahoo Will Delete All Yahoo Groups Content on
December 14th." Verge, December 16, 2019, https://www
.theverge.com/2019/10/16/20917710/yahoo-groups-deleting
-all-content-upload-message-boards-email-communities.

Popper, Ben. "Nextdoor—A Private, Localized Social Network—Is
Now Used in Over 100,000 US Neighborhoods." Verge, June 23,
2016, https://www.theverge.com/2016/6/23/12005456/nextdoor
-100000-neighborhood-social-network-app-changes-business
-plan-expansion.

Preece, Jenny, and Diane Maloney-Krichmar. "Online Communities: Design, Theory, and Practice." *Journal of Computer-Mediated Communication* 10, no. 4 (July 2005).

Pritchard, Stephen. "The Readers' Editor on . . . Handling Comments Below the Line." *Guardian*, January 31, 2016, https://www .theguardian.com/commentisfree/2016/jan/31/readers-editor -on-readers-comments-below-the-line.

"Promote Local Business and Commerce the Right Way." Nextdoor, https://help.nextdoor.com/s/article/promote-local-business -and-commerce-the-right-way?language=en_US.

Putnam, Robert D. *Bowling Alone: The Collapse and Revival of American Community*. New York: Simon & Schuster, 2000.

Rahn, Will. "Steve Bannon and the Alt-Right: A Primer." CBS News, August 19, 2016, https://www.cbsnews.com/news/steve-bannon -and-the-alt-right-a-primer.

Rao, Leena. "Yahoo Quietly Pulls the Plug on Geocities." *TechCrunch*, April 23, 2009, https://www.techcrunch.com /2009/04/23/yahoo-quietly-pulls-the-plug-on-geocities/.

Romano, Aja. "A New Law Intended to Curb Sex Trafficking Threatens the Future of the Internet as We Know It." *Vox*, July 2, 2018, https://www.vox.com/culture/2018/4/13/17172762 /fosta-sesta-backpage-230-internet-freedom.

Rovzar, Chris. "Unpaid *Huffington Post* Bloggers: 'Hey, Arianna, Can You Spare a Dime?'" *Intelligencer*, February 10, 2011, http://www.nymag .com/intelligencer/2011/02/unpaid_huffington_post_blogger.html.

Sakuma, Amanda. "Sacramento Police Officers Will Not Be Charged for Fatally Shooting Stephon Clark." *Vox*, March 3,

2019, https://www.vox.com/2019/3/3/18248625/stephon-clark
-sacramento-police-officers-shooting.

Schindler, Philipp. "Expanded Safeguards for Advertisers." *Google*
(blog), March 21, 2017, https://blog.google/topics/ads
/expanded-safeguards-for-advertisers/.

Schneider, Avie. "Twitter Bans Alex Jones and InfoWars; Cites
Abusive Behavior." NPR, September 6, 2018, https://www.npr
.org/2018/09/06/645352618/twitter-bans-alex-jones-and
-infowars-cites-abusive-behavior.

Schwartz, Mattathias. "Facebook Failed to Protect 30 Million
Users from Having Their Data Harvested by Trump Campaign
Affiliate." *Intercept*, March 30, 2017, https://www.theintercept
.com/2017/03/30/facebook-failed-to-protect-30-million-users
-from-having-their-data-harvested-by-trump-campaign
-affiliate/.

Seering, J., Tony Wang, Jina Yoon, and Geoff Kaufman. "Moderator
Engagement and Community Development in the Age of
Algorithms." *New Media & Society* 21, no. 7 (2019): 1–28; https://
www.andrew.cmu.edu/user/jseering/papers/Seering%20et%20
al%202019%20Moderators.pdf.

Seltzer, Sarah. "3 Million of Hillary's Biggest Supporters Found Each
Other in a Secret Facebook Group." *Nation*, November 17, 2016,
https://www.thenation.com/article/3-million-of-hillarys-biggest
-supporters-found-each-other-in-a-secret-facebook-group/.

Sherr, Ian. "Discord, Slack for Gamers, Tops 250 Million Registered
Users." CNET, May 13, 2019, https://www.cnet.com/g00/news
/discord-slack-for-gamers-hits-its-fourth-year-at-250-million
-registered-users/?i10c.encReferrer=aHR0cHM6Ly93d3cuZ29vZ
2xlLmNvbS8%3d.

Sleeping Giants. "SG CONFIRMED LIST 05/03/2019." https://docs
.google.com/spreadsheets/d/1i9o8CR_kjJ6mBd44k6CRZEhl
XuZqq-XCCOoj-e8RJ7Q/edit#gid=0.

"Starbucks and Walmart Join Growing List of Advertisers
Boycotting YouTube." *Guardian*, March 24, 2017, https://www
.theguardian.com/technology/2017/mar/24/walmart
-starbucks-pepsi-pull-ads-google-youtube.

Statt, Nick. "Mark Zuckerberg Just Unveiled Facebook's New Mission
Statement." *Verge*, June 22, 2017, https://www.theverge
.com/2017/6/22/15855202/facebook-ceo-mark-zuckerberg
-new-mission-statement-groups.

Statt, Nick. "*World of Warcraft* Is Dominating Twitch Because
Fortnite Streamers Are Desperate for Change." *Verge*, September
11, 2019, https://www.theverge.com/2019/9/11/20861066/world-of
-warcraft-wow-classic-twitch-fortnite-ninja-streamers-change.

Stephen, Bijan. "Some of the UK's Phone Number Infrastructure
Relies on Yahoo Groups, Which Is Shutting Down." *Verge*,
October 17, 2019, https://www.theverge.com/2019/10/17/20919630
/yahoo-groups-uk-ofcom-simwood-numbers.

Stites, Tom. "About 1,300 U.S. Communities Have Totally Lost News
Coverage, UNC News Desert Study Finds." *Poynter*, October
15, 2018, https://www.poynter.org/business-work/2018
/about-1300-u-s-communities-have-totally-lost-news-coverage
-unc-news-desert-study-finds/.

Stop Enabling Sex Traffickers Act of 2017, S. 1693, 115th Cong. (2017–
2018), https://www.congress.gov/bill/115th-congress/senate
-bill/1693.

Taylor, Jessica. "Energized by Trump's Win, White Nationalists
Gather to 'Change the World,'" NPR, November 20, 2016,

https://www.npr.org/2016/11/20/502719871/energized-by
-trumps-win-white-nationalists-gather-to-change-the-world.

"The Conversation Starts Here." Reddit, https://www.redditinc.com/.

"The Story of Patreon." Patreon, https://www.patreon.com/about.

Thursten, Chris. "*Star Wars Galaxies* Was an MMO That Almost
Changed the World." *PC Gamer*, January 25, 2019, https://
www.pcgamer.com/star-wars-galaxies-was-an-mmo-that
-almost-changed-the-world/.

"Troll Patrol Findings." Amnesty International, https://decoders
.amnesty.org/projects/troll-patrol/findings#introduction.

Tufekci, Zeynep. *Twitter and Tear Gas: The Power and Fragility of
Networked Protest.* New Haven, CT: Yale University Press, 2017.

Waddell, Kaveh. "The Police Officer 'Nextdoor.'" *Atlantic*, May 4, 2016,
https://www.theatlantic.com/technology/archive/2016/05
/nextdoor-social-network-police-seattle/481164/.

"We Built Discord to Bring Gamers Together." Discord, https://
discordapp.com/company.

"We Only Succeed When You Succeed." Patreon, https://www
.patreon.com/product/pricing.

Wiener, Anna. "The Lonely Work of Moderating Hacker News." *New
Yorker*, August 8, 2019, https://www.newyorker.com/news/letter
-from-silicon-valley/the-lonely-work-of-moderating-hacker-news.

Woolf, Nicky. "Destroyer of Worlds." Tortoise, June 29, 2019, https://
members.tortoisemedia.com/2019/06/29/8chan/content.html.

"*World of Warcraft* Classic: Hit Game Goes Back to Basics." BBC,
August 26, 2019, https://www.bbc.com/news/technology
-49448935.

Notes

Introduction:
Why Moderators Matter

1. Jenny Preece and Diane Maloney-Krichmar, "Online Communities: Design, Theory, and Practice," *Journal of Computer-Mediated Communication* 10, no. 4 (July 2005).
2. Ibid.
3. Brian Butler, Lee Sproull, Sara Kiesler, and Robert Kraut, "Community Effort in Online Groups: Who Does the Work and Why?" in Susan Weisband, ed., *Leadership at a Distance: Research in Technologically-Supported Work* (New York: Lawrence Erlbaum Associates, 2008), 173.
4. Ibid., 188.
5. Claudia Lo, "When All You Have Is a Banhammer: The Social and Communicative Work of Volunteer Moderators," master's degree dissertation, Massachusetts Institute of Technology, 2018, p. 24.
6. Ibid., 11.
7. Adrian Chen, "When the Internet's 'Moderators' Are Anything But," *New York Times Magazine*, July 21, 2015, https://www.nytimes.com/2015/07/26/magazine/when -the-internets-moderators-are-anything-but.html.
8. Casey Newton, "The Trauma Floor: The Secret Lives of Facebook Moderators in America," *Verge*, February 25, 2019,

https://www.theverge.com/2019/2/25/18229714
/cognizant-facebook-content-moderator-interviews
-trauma-working-conditions-arizona.

9. Self-described furries enjoy anthropomorphized animals. The fandom sometimes includes creating art or dressing up in costumes. The Discord controversy is summarized in an article by Steven Asarch in *Newsweek*: "Discord Comes Under Fire for Alleged Moderator Abuse and Furry Corruption," https://www .newsweek.com/discord-furries-terms-service-community -guidelines-1323099.

Chapter 1:
Building Bridges: Make America Dinner Again

1. Peter Levine, "How to Respond," November 11, 2016, http:// peterlevine.ws/images/Screen-Shot-2016-11-11-at-1.19.30 -PM-1.png.

2. Pew Research Center, "Partisanship and Political Animosity in 2016," June 22, 2016, https://www.people-press.org/2016/06 /22/partisanship-and-political-animosity-in-2016/.

3. Ibid.

4. Shanto Iyengar, Yphtach Lelkes, Matthew Levendusky, Neil Malhotra, and Sean J. Westwood, "The Origins and Consequences of Affective Polarization in the United States," *Annual Review of Political Science* 22, no. 1 (May 11, 2019): 143; https://www-annualreviews-org.proxyau.wrlc.org/doi/10.1146 /annurev-polisci-051117-073034.

5. "Blue Feed, Red Feed," *Wall Street Journal*, last updated August 19, 2019, http://graphics.wsj.com/blue-feed-red-feed/.

6. Ricardo Bilton, "The Wall Street Journal's New Tool Gives a Side-by-Side Look at the Facebook Political News Filter Bubble," NiemanLab, May 18, 2016, https://www.niemanlab

.org/2016/05/the-wall-street-journals-new-tool-gives-a-side
-by-side-look-at-the-facebook-political-news-filter-bubble/.

7. Robert D. Putnam, *Bowling Alone: The Collapse and Revival of American Community* (New York: Simon & Schuster, 2000), 100.

8. Iyengar, Lelkes, Levendusky, Malhotra, and Westwood, "The Origins and Consequences of Affective Polarization in the United States," 140.

9. Douglas J. Ahler, "Self-Fulfilling Misperceptions of Public Polarization," *Journal of Politics* 76, no. 3 (2014): 607–20; doi:10.1017/s0022381614000085.

10. Mattathias Schwartz, "Facebook Failed to Protect 30 Million Users from Having Their Data Harvested by Trump Campaign Affiliate," *Intercept*, March 30, 2017, https://theintercept.com /2017/03/30/facebook-failed-to-protect-30-million-users-from -having-their-data-harvested-by-trump-campaign-affiliate/.

11. Nick Statt, "Mark Zuckerberg Just Unveiled Facebook's New Mission Statement," *Verge*, June 22, 2017, https://www.theverge .com/2017/6/22/15855202/facebook-ceo-mark-zuckerberg -new-mission-statement-groups.

12. Heather Kelly, "Mark Zuckerberg Explains Why He Just Changed Facebook's Mission," CNN Money, June 22, 2017, https://money.cnn.com/2017/06/22/technology/facebook -zuckerberg-interview/index.html.

13. J. B. Thompson, *The Media and Modernity: A Social Theory of the Media*, as cited by Anika Gupta, "Towards a Better Inclusivity: Online Comments and Community at News Organizations," master's degree dissertation, Massachusetts Institute of Technology, 2016.

14. J. Seering, Tony Wang, Jina Yoon, and Geoff Kaufman, "Moderator Engagement and Community Development in the Age of Algorithms," *New Media & Society* 21, no. 7 (2019): 16;

https://www.andrew.cmu.edu/user/jseering/papers/Seering%20et%20al%202019%20Moderators.pdf.

15. Ahler, "Self-Fulfilling Misperceptions of Public Polarization," 608.

16. Ibid., 610.

17. David Brooks, "Why Trump Voters Stick with Him," *New York Times*, October 3, 2019, https://www.nytimes.com/2019/10/03/opinion/trump-voters.html.

18. Anna Wiener, "The Lonely Work of Moderating Hacker News," *New Yorker*, August 8, 2019, https://www.newyorker.com/news/letter-from-silicon-valley/the-lonely-work-of-moderating-hacker-news.

19. Jane Jacobs, Paul Kuhne, and C. J. Peek, "Participant-Identified Effects of Better Angels Experiences," Better Angels, October 2019, https://drive.google.com/file/d/1kkpwt59p7Ci6jhtOaAlYFr0cqy4QOAy9/view.

Chapter 2
Hard Conversations: Pantsuit Nation and Real Talk

1. Gupta, "Towards a Better Inclusivity."

2. Stephen Pritchard, "The Readers' Editor on . . . Handling Comments Below the Line," *Guardian*, January 31, 2016, https://www.theguardian.com/commentisfree/2016/jan/31/readers-editor-on-readers-comments-below-the-line.

3. Juliana Menasce Horowitz, Anna Brown, and Kiana Cox, "Race in America 2019," Pew Research Center, April 9, 2019, https://www.pewsocialtrends.org/2019/04/09/race-in-america-2019/.

4. Sarah Seltzer, "3 Million of Hillary's Biggest Supporters Found Each Other in a Secret Facebook Group," *Nation*, November 17, 2016, https://www.thenation.com/article/3-million-of-hillarys-biggest-supporters-found-each-other-in-a-secret-facebook-group/.

5. Alexandra Alter, "A Book Deal for Pantsuit Nation, and Then a Backlash," *New York Times*, December 21, 2016, https://www.nytimes.com/2016/12/21/business/a-book-deal-for-pantsuit-nation-and-then-a-backlash.html.

6. Libby Chamberlain, ed., *Pantsuit Nation* (New York: Flatiron Books, 2017), xvii.

7. Seltzer, "3 Million of Hillary's Biggest Supporters."

8. Jenina Marie, "Open Letter to Pantsuit Nation," *Smart Media Mom* (blog), December 3, 2016, https://smartmediamom.com/2016/12/03/open-letter-to-pantsuit-nation/.

9. Harry Lewis, "Pantsuit Nation Is a Sham," *Huffington Post*, December 20, 2016, https://www.huffpost.com/entry/pantsuit-nation-is-a-sham_b_585991dce4b04d7df167cb4d.

10. Gupta, "Towards a Better Inclusivity."

11. Ibid.

12. "Troll Patrol Findings," Amnesty International, https://decoders.amnesty.org/projects/troll-patrol/findings#introduction.

13. Lecia Michelle, "Nonblack POC, Stop Acting Like Black Women Are Invincible and Don't Feel Pain," *Medium*, June 18, 2018, https://medium.com/@LeciaMichelle/nonblack-poc-stop-acting-like-black-women-are-invincible-and-dont-feel-pain-803970064ef4.

14. Lecia Michelle, "White Women Can't Even Commit to a 2-Week Racial Justice Mentoring Class," *Medium*, November 25, 2018, https://medium.com/@LeciaMichelle/white-women-cant-even-commit-to-a-2-week-racial-justice-mentoring-class-fd58049d3633.

15. Jonah Engel Bromwich, "Can Society Scale?" *New York Times*, August 10, 2018, https://www.nytimes.com/2018/08/10/style/numtot-urbanism-memes.html.

16. Nancy Fraser, "Rethinking the Public Sphere: A Contribution to the Critique of Actually Existing Democracy," *Social Text* 25/26 (January 1, 1990): 70.

Chapter 3:
All in the Neighborhood: Nextdoors, NUMTOTs, and More

1. 2010–2014 ACS 5-Year Estimates Ward 3, Office of Planning, August 9, 2016, https://planning.dc.gov/node/1180945.

2. Jay Peters, "Yahoo Will Delete All Yahoo Groups Content on December 14th," Verge, October 16, 2019, https://www .theverge.com/2019/10/16/20917710/yahoo-groups-deleting -all-content-upload-message-boards-email-communities.

3. Bijan Stephen, "Some of the UK's Phone Number Infrastructure Relies on Yahoo Groups, Which Is Shutting Down," Verge, October 17, 2019, https://www.theverge.com/2019/10/17 /20919630/yahoo-groups-uk-ofcom-simwood-numbers.

4. Jordan Pearson, "Yahoo Groups Is Winding Down and All Content Will Be Permanently Removed," Vice, October 16, 2019, https://www.vice.com/en_us/article/8xwe9p/yahoo -groups-is-winding-down-and-all-content-will-be-permanently -removed.

5. Leena Rao, "Yahoo Quietly Pulls the Plug on Geocities," TechCrunch, April 23, 2009, https://techcrunch.com/2009 /04/23/yahoo-quietly-pulls-the-plug-on-geocities/.

6. Terence McCoy, "Georgetown Social Network Accused of Racial Profiling Is Suspended," Washington Post, October 19, 2015, https://www.washingtonpost.com/local/georgetown -social-network-accused-of-racial-profiling-is-suspended /2015/10/19/7a8865a2-7674-11e5-b9c1-f03c48c96ac2 _story.html.

7. Jennifer Medina, "Website Meant to Connect Neighbors Hears Complaints of Racial Profiling," New York Times, May 18, 2016, https://www.nytimes.com/2016/05/19/us /website-nextdoor-hears-racial-profiling-complaints .html.

8. Tom Stites, "About 1,300 U.S. Communities Have Totally Lost News Coverage, UNC News Desert Study Finds," *Poynter*, October 15, 2018, https://www.poynter.org /business-work/2018/about-1300-u-s-communities-have -totally-lost-news-coverage-unc-news-desert-study-finds/.

9. Ben Popper, "Nextdoor—a Private, Localized Social Network— Is Now Used in Over 100,000 US Neighborhoods," *Verge*, June 23, 2016, https://www.theverge.com/2016/6/23 /12005456/nextdoor-100000-neighborhood-social-network -app-changes-business-plan-expansion.

10. "About Us," Nextdoor, https://about.nextdoor.com/gb/.

11. Kaveh Waddell, "The Police Officer 'Nextdoor,'" *Atlantic*, May 4, 2016, https://www.theatlantic.com/technology/archive /2016/05/nextdoor-social-network-police-seattle/481164/.

12. "About Nextdoor Leads," Nextdoor, https://help.nextdoor .com/s/article/About-Nextdoor-Leads?language=en_US.

13. "Promote Local Business and Commerce the Right Way," Nextdoor, https://help.nextdoor.com/s/article/promote-local -business-and-commerce-the-right-way?language=en_US.

14. "Crime or Suspicious Activity," Nextdoor, https://help .nextdoor.com/s/article/be-helpful-not-hurtful?language =en_US#5.

15. Christina Masden, Catherine Grevet, Rebecca Grinter, Eric Gilbert, and W. Keith Edwards, "Tensions in Scaling-up Community Social Media: A Multi-Neighborhood Study of Nextdoor," School of Interactive Computing and GVU Center, Georgia Institute of Technology, https://www.cc.gatech.edu /~keith/pubs/nextdoor-chi2014.pdf.

16. Richard Florida, "Young People's Love of Cities Isn't a Passing Fad," *CityLab*, May 28, 2019, https://www.citylab.com/life /2019/05/urban-living-housing-choices-millennials-move -to-research/590347/.

17. Andrew Killian, "What's Driving Growth in Urban Planning Degrees?" Data USA, April 3, 2016, https://datausa.io /story/04-04-2016_urban-planning-degrees.

18. Masden, Grevet, Grinter, Gilbert, and Edwards, "Tensions in Scaling-up Community Social Media."

19. Jonah Engel Bromwich, "Can Society Scale?" *New York Times*, August 10, 2018, https://www.nytimes.com/2018/08 /10/style/numtot-urbanism-memes.html.

20. Ibid.

21. Bryan Dosono and Bryan Semaan, "Moderation Practices as Emotional Labor in Sustaining Online Communities: The Case of AAPI Identity Work on Reddit," *CHI '19: Proceedings of the 2019 CHI Conference on Human Factors in Computing Systems*, paper no. 142, May 2019, https://dl.acm.org/citation.cfm?id=3300372.

22. Ibid., 6–7.

23. Lisa Margonelli, "Inside AOL's 'Cyber-Sweatshop,'" *Wired*, October 1, 1999, https://www.wired.com/1999/10/volunteers/.

24. Alex Mayyasi, "The AOL Chat Room Monitor Revolt," *Priceonomics*, August 21, 2014, https://priceonomics.com /the-aol-chat-room-monitor-revolt/.

25. Brian Lynch and Courtney Swearingen, "Why We Shut Down Reddit's 'Ask Me Anything' Forum," *New York Times*, July 8, 2015, https://www.nytimes.com/2015/07/08/opinion /why-we-shut-down-reddits-ask-me-anything-forum.html.

26. Chris Rovzar, "Unpaid Huffington Post Bloggers: 'Hey, Arianna, Can You Spare a Dime?'" *Intelligencer*, February 10, 2011, http://nymag.com/intelligencer/2011/02/unpaid _huffington_post_blogger.html.

27. Casey Newton, "Bodies in Seats," *Verge*, June 19, 2019, https://www.theverge.com/2019/6/19/18681845/facebook -moderator-interviews-video-trauma-ptsd-cognizant-tampa.

28. Ibid.

29. Newton, "The Trauma Floor."

30. Panchalay Chalermkraivuth, "'She Can Lead. She Can Live.' Black Women's March Draws Hundreds to State Capitol," *Sacramento Bee*, June 22, 2019, https://www .sacbee.com/news/local/article231865683.html.

31. Amanda Sakuma, "Sacramento Police Officers Will Not Be Charged for Fatally Shooting Stephon Clark," *Vox*, March 3, 2019, https://www.vox.com/2019/3/3/18248625 /stephon-clark-sacramento-police-officers-shooting.

32. Kerra L. Bolton, "Stephon Clark's Tweets Are a Reminder: #SayHerName," CNN, April 19, 2018, https://www.cnn.com /2018/04/19/opinions/stephon-clark-tweets-hurt-women -bolton-opinion/index.html.

Chapter 4
Bringing the Revolution:
Sleeping Giants and the Battle over Online Advertising

1. Sapna Maheshwari, "Revealed: The People Behind an Anti- Breitbart Twitter Account," *New York Times*, July 20, 2018, https://www.nytimes.com/2018/07/20/business/media /sleeping-giants-breitbart-twitter.html.

2. Joshua A. Braun, John D. Coakley, and Emily West, "Activism, Advertising, and Far-Right Media: The Case of Sleeping Giants," *Media and Communication 7*, no. 4 (December 2019): 68–79, doi:10.17645.

3. Lauren Fisher, "US Programmatic Ad Spending Forecast 2019," Emarketer.com, April 25, 2019, https://www.emarketer .com/content/us-programmatic-ad-spending-forecast-2019.

4. IAB Europe, "The Current State of the Programmatic Advertising Market," March 21, 2019, https://iabeurope.eu/blog/the -current-state-of-the-programmatic-advertising-market.

5. Braun, Coakley, and West, "Activism, Advertising, and Far-Right Media," 70.

6. Abha Bhattarai, "Breitbart Lost 90 Percent of Its Advertisers in Two Months: Who's Still There?" *Washington Post*, June 8, 2017, https://www.washingtonpost.com/news/business/wp/2017/06/08/breitbart-lost-90-percent-of-its-advertisers-in-two-months-whos-still-there/.

7. Braun, Coakley, and West, "Activism, Advertising, and Far-Right Media," 69.

8. Will Rahn, "Steve Bannon and the Alt-Right: A Primer," CBS News, August 19, 2016, https://www.cbsnews.com/news/steve-bannon-and-the-alt-right-a-primer.

9. Callum Borchers, "'Can You Name One White Nationalist Article at Breitbart?' Challenge Accepted!" *Washington Post*, November 15, 2016, https://www.washingtonpost.com/news/the-fix/wp/2016/11/15/can-you-name-one-white-nationalist-article-at-breitbart-challenge-accepted/.

10. Jessica Taylor, "Energized by Trump's Win, White Nationalists Gather To 'Change the World,'" NPR, November 20, 2016, https://www.npr.org/2016/11/20/502719871/energized-by-trumps-win-white-nationalists-gather-to-change-the-world.

11. Michael M. Grynbaum and John Herrman, "Breitbart Rises from Outlier to Potent Voice in Campaign," *New York Times*, August 26, 2016, https://www.nytimes.com/2016/08/27/business/media/breitbart-news-presidential-race.html.

12. David Ng, "Chick-fil-A Will Stop Donating to Salvation Army, Christian Athletes Following LGBT Pressure," Breitbart, November 18, 2019, https://www.breitbart.com/tech/2019/11/18/chick-fil-a-will-stop-donating-to-salvation-army-christian-athletes-following-lgbt-pressure/.

13. Sean Captain, "Disqus Grapples with Hosting Toxic Comments on Breitbart and Extreme-Right Sites," *Fast*

Company, March 8, 2017, https://www.fastcompany.com /3068698/disqus-grapples-with-hosting-toxic-comments -on-breitbart-and-extreme-right-sites.

14. Nandini Jammi, "PPC Marketers: Don't Wait for Permission to Blacklist Breitbart News," *Medium*, November 23, 2016, https:// medium.com/@nandoodles/ppc-marketers-dont-wait -for-permission-to-blacklist-breitbart-news-83872c2a7442.

15. Maria Perez, "Steve Bannon Out at Breitbart: Seven Most Controversial Articles Published by Trump's Former Aide," *Newsweek*, January 9, 2018, https://www.newsweek.com /steve-bannon-breitbart-trump-controversial-776262.

16. Breitbart Tech, "Would You Rather Your Child Had Feminism or Cancer?" Breitbart, February 19, 2016, https://www.breitbart .com/clips/2016/02/19/would-you-rather-your-child-had -feminism-or-cancer/.

17. Sleeping Giants, "SG CONFIRMED LIST 05/03/2019," https://docs.google.com/spreadsheets/d/1i9o8CR _kjJ6mBd44k6CRZEhlXuZqq-XCCOoj-e8RJ7Q/edit#gid=0.

18. Katrina Stirton Dodd, "Cannes Lions: Social & Influencer Winners 2019," Contagious, June 19, 2019, https://www .contagious.com/news-and-views/cannes-lions-winners-2019 -social-influencer-category.

19. Justin Caruso, "'Non-Political' Sleeping Giants Repeatedly Go after Steve King, Endorse Democrat Opponent," Breitbart, October 24, 2018, https://www.breitbart.com/tech/2018 /10/24/non-political-sleeping-giants-repeatedly-go-after -steve-king-endorse-democrat-opponent/.

20. Milo, "Gawker: 'Dishonest Fascists' of GamerGate Could Cost Us 'Millions,'" Breitbart, October 23, 2014, https:// www.breitbart.com/europe/2014/10/23/gawker-dishonest -fascists-of-gamergate-could-cost-us-millions.

21. Breitbart News, "#Dumpkelloggs: Breakfast Brand Blacklists

Breitbart, Declares Hate for 45,000,000 Readers," Breitbart, November 30, 2016, https://www.breitbart.com/politics /2016/11/30/dumpkelloggs-kelloggs-declares-hate-45-million -americans-blacklisting-breitbart/.

22. Alexi Mostrous, "Big Brands Fund Terror through Online Adverts," *The Times*, February 9, 2017, https://www.thetimes .co.uk/article/big-brands-fund-terror-knnxfgb98.

23. "Starbucks and Walmart Join Growing List of Advertisers Boycotting YouTube," *Guardian*, March 25, 2017, https://www .theguardian.com/technology/2017/mar/24/walmart -starbucks-pepsi-pull-ads-google-youtube.

24. Ronan Harris, "Improving Our Brand Safety Controls," *Google* (blog), March 17, 2017, https://blog.google/topics /google-europe/improving-our-brand-safety-controls/.

25. Philipp Schindler, "Expanded Safeguards for Advertisers," *Google* (blog), March 21, 2017, https://blog.google /topics/ads/expanded-safeguards-for-advertisers/.

26. Anatoliy Gruzd, Barry Wellman, and Yuri Takhteyev, "Imagining Twitter as an Imagined Community," *American Behavioral Scientist* 55, no. 10 (July 25, 2011): 3; https:// journals.sagepub.com/doi/abs/10.1177/0002764211409378.

27. Avie Schneider, "Twitter Bans Alex Jones and InfoWars; Cites Abusive Behavior," NPR, September 6, 2018, https://www.npr .org/2018/09/06/645352618/twitter-bans-alex-jones-and -infowars-cites-abusive-behavior.

28. An alias used to protect her identity, as she is anonymous.

29. Braun, Coakley, and West, "Activism, Advertising, and Far-Right Media," 76.

Chapter 5

Playing the Game: Keeping the Fun in MMORPGs

1. Ian Sherr, "Discord, Slack for Gamers, Tops 250 Million Registered Users," CNET, May 13, 2019, https://www .cnet.com/g00/news/discord-slack-for-gamers-hits-its -fourth-year-at-250-million-registered-users/?i10c.enc Referrer=aHR0cHM6Ly93d3cuZ29vZ2xlLmNvbS8%3d.

2. Henry Jenkins, "Video Games Myths Revisited: New Pew Study Tells Us about Games and Youth," *Confessions of an Aca-Fan* (blog), October 2, 2008, http://henryjenkins.org /blog/2008/10/video_games_myths_revisited_ne.html.

3. Activision Blizzard, Inc., "Activision Blizzard Announces Record Fourth Quarter and Full Year Earnings Per Share," investor news release, February 5, 2015, https://investor.activision .com/static-files/31066916-9fc0-49bf-9914-553661592dee.

4. "World of Warcraft Classic: Hit Game Goes Back to Basics," BBC, August 26, 2019, https://www.bbc.com/news/technology -49448935.

5. This claim is not hugely controversial, but it's also not officially verified. Articles in gaming news outlets and those written by fans regularly list *WoW* as having the largest MMORPG player base in the world.

6. Nick Statt, "World of Warcraft Is Dominating Twitch Because Fortnite Streamers Are Desperate for Change," *Verge*, September 11, 2019, https://www.theverge.com/2019/9/11 /20861066/world-of-warcraft-wow-classic-twitch-fortnite -ninja-streamers-change.

7. "We Built Discord to Bring Gamers Together," Discord, https://discordapp.com/company.

8. Chris Thursten, "Star Wars Galaxies Was an MMO That Almost Changed the World," *PC Gamer*, January 25, 2019,

https://www.pcgamer.com/star-wars-galaxies-was-an
-mmo-that-almost-changed-the-world/.

9. Ben Barrett, "1,960 Man-Hours per Week: The Truth about
WoW Raiding at the Highest Level," *PCGamesN*, https://www
.pcgamesn.com/world-of-warcraft/wow-raiding-nighthold
-method-danish-terrace-death-jesters.

10. For more discussion on emotional labor, see chapter three,
"All in the Neighborhood."

11. Julie Beck, "The Concept Creep of 'Emotional Labor,'" *Atlantic*,
November 26, 2018, https://www.theatlantic.com/family
/archive/2018/11/arlie-hochschild-housework-isnt-emotional
-labor/576637/.

12. Icarus Twine is an online alias, and the name he asked to be
identified by here.

13. In case it's not obvious, this is a screen name, which is what
he asked me to use.

Chapter 6
For All the World to See: Moderating Reddit

1. Reseph is one of the names he uses online, and the one he
asked to be identified by here.

2. "The Conversation Starts Here," Reddit, https://www.redditinc
.com/.

3. "Wikimedia Statistics," Wikimedia, https://stats.wikimedia
.org/v2/#/all-projects.

4. Chen, "When the Internet's 'Moderators' Are Anything But."

5. Adrian Chen, "Unmasking Reddit's Violentacrez, the Biggest
Troll on the Web," *Gawker*, October 12, 2012, https://gawker
.com/5950981/unmasking-reddits-violentacrez-the-biggest
-troll-on-the-web.

6. J. Nathan Matias, "Preventing Harassment and Increasing Group Participation through Social Norms in 2,190 Online Science Discussions," *PNAS* 116, no. 20 (May 14, 2019), https://www.pnas.org/content/pnas/116/20/9785.full.pdf.

7. A "free company" is the *FFXIV* term for a group of people who regularly play together, similar to a "guild" in *World of Warcraft*.

8. Jialun "Aaron" Jiang, Charles Kiene, Skylar Middler, Jed. R. Brubaker, and Casey Fiesler, "Moderation Challenges in Voice-Based Online Communities on Discord," *Proceedings of the ACM on Human-Computer Interaction* 3, no. CSCW, article 55 (November 2019), https://aaronjiang .me/assets/bibliography/pdf/cscw2019-discord.pdf.

9. Ibid.

10. Jialun "Aaron" Jiang, "Voice-Based Communities and Why It's So Hard to Moderate Them," *ACM CSCW* (blog), *Medium*, August 29, 2019, https://medium.com/acm-cscw/voice-based -communities-and-why-they-are-so-hard-to-moderate -b3339c1f0f6a.

Chapter 7
Building a Creative Community: The Artists of YouTube

1. The name he uses for his online work, and the one he asked me to use in this book.

2. "The Story of Patreon," Patreon, https://www.patreon.com /about.

3. "We Only Succeed When You Succeed," Patreon, https://www .patreon.com/product/pricing.

Chapter 8
Out of the Darkness: Kink and FetLife

1. As of December 2019.
2. In case it's not obvious, this is a screen name. It's the same one he uses online while moderating his community, and the one he asked me to use in this book.
3. These questions are paraphrased examples of common questions.
4. Allow States and Victims to Fight Online Sex Trafficking Act of 2017, HR 1865, 115th Cong. (2017–2018), https://www.congress.gov/bill/115th-congress/senate-bill/1693.
5. Aja Romano, "A New Law Intended to Curb Sex Trafficking Threatens the Future of the Internet as We Know It," Vox, July 2, 2018, https://www.vox.com/culture/2018/4/13/17172762/fosta-sesta-backpage-230-internet-freedom.
6. "About FOSTA," Craigslist, https://www.craigslist.org/about/FOSTA.
7. This text is his example; not all the new arrivals were coming from Cleveland.
8. Emma Green, "Consent Isn't Enough: The Troubling Sex of Fifty Shades," Atlantic, February 10, 2015, https://www.theatlantic.com/entertainment/archive/2015/02/consent-isnt-enough-in-fifty-shades-of-grey/385267/.
9. His example!

Index

Wikipedia, 131
Wired, 76
Women's March on Washington,
    9, 82
Workable, 85–86
World of Warcraft (WoW), 107–27, 186
    Bring the C'Thunder guild,
        118–25
    dungeons, 109, 111, 126–27
    growth and size of, 110, 121
    guild administrator roles and
        responsibilities, 108–10,
        114–16, 123–24
    guild leader roles and
        responsibilities, 111–13, 115–27
    guilds/player cooperatives, 109
    keyboard shortcuts, 108–9
    Method guild, 116
    new players, 107–9, 112, 114, 121,
        126–27
    origins of, 110
    rules and guidelines, 116–18, 186
    Terminus guild, 109, 111–16

Y
Yahoo:
    and moderators of large groups,
        60
    ONElist acquisition, 60
    shutdown of GeoCities, 62
    Yahoo Groups, 60–62

Yiannopoulos, Milo, 92
YouTube, 145–57
    advertising revenue, 151
    comments section, xix–xx, xxviii,
        148–50, 155–57, 187
    content-tagging algorithm,
        151–52
    copyright protections, xviii,
        151–52
    Discord community site and,
        150, 153–57, 182–83, 187
    influencers, xii
    and *Marble Hornets* (web horror
        series), 145–51
    and moderators of large groups,
        xiii
    Night Mind channel, 145–57, 187
    Nick Nocturne (YouTube creator),
        145–57, 187
    paid/contract moderators, 28
    Patreon (creator site) and, xviii,
        150, 152–57, 183
    subscribing to, ix–x
    terrorism and, 93–94
    Tumblr and, 148, 150–51, 153, 155
    tutorials, 148
    Twitter and, 146–48, 150, 151, 155
    vlogs, 148

Z
Zuckerberg, Mark, 12, 96

About the Author

Anika Gupta is a digital thought leader whose research on online communities spans several industries. A former science and technology journalist, she's currently a senior product manager at the *Atlantic*. In 2019, she was honored as a member of the Online News Association's Women's Leadership Accelerator, a program that finds and trains women media leaders for roles as leaders in the industry. She has a master's degree in comparative media studies from the Massachusetts Institute of Technology and a bachelor's degree in journalism from the Medill School of Journalism at Northwestern University. Her journalistic work has appeared online in *Smithsonian*, *Fortune*, the *Guardian*, and elsewhere.